MONEY

The wise sage and
the money journey

Sam Gray

© Copyright Sam Gray, 2017

Edited by Rebekah Groves

Formats available: Paperback; eBook

ISBN: 978-0-646-97180-3

At the time of writing it is believed that the information within this book is accurate and up to date. Every attempt has been made to ensure its accuracy and relevance, however no guarantee is made of this. Please be aware that rules and regulations are subject to change, and should you be reading this sometime after it has been published, rules and regulations may have changed.

The information provided in this book (including taxation) is general in nature and does not consider your individual circumstances or needs. Before acting on this information you should consider its appropriateness, having regard to your own objectives, financial situation and needs. Where applicable, you should read the relevant product disclosure statement and seek personal advice from a qualified financial adviser.

The views expressed in this publication are solely those of the author; they are not reflective or indicative of Millennium3 Financial Service's position, and are not to be attributed to Millennium3. They cannot be reproduced in any form without the express written consent of the author.

This book is intended to provide a starting point in improving your financial affairs. It by no means replaces the need for professional advice.

Sam Gray

contact address: PO Box 266 Subiaco WA 6904

contact email: samg@incitowealth.com.au

Dedication

I am deeply grateful for the love, support and kindness of my family and girlfriend who have helped shape me as the person I am today.

To anyone who wants to get ahead financially, may this book inspire you to better things.

Table of Contents

Introduction 7
The journey begins 7

Chapter One Being mindful with money 13
    Lesson One: Your money psychology and money habits 13

Chapter Two Setting the path 25
    Lesson Two: Goal setting 25

Chapter Three Building wealth 33
    Lesson Three: Reaching financial security and financial freedom 33
    Lesson Four: Effectively building wealth 37
    Lesson Five: Building wealth through a business 49

Chapter Four Deep dive into investing 55
    Lesson Six: More about investing 55
    Lesson Seven: Things to know for constructing an investment portfolio 60
    Lesson Eight: Things to consider in buying a home 75

Chapter Five Retirement and superannuation 83
    Lesson Nine: Retirement planning system – Superannuation 83
    Lesson Ten: How much is enough for retirement? 88

Chapter Six Family-related planning 93
    Lesson Eleven: Giving your kids a head-start with money 93

    Lesson Twelve: Protecting your family 96
    Lesson Thirteen: Estate planning 100

Putting it all together 107

Bonus Chapter 111

Risks to retirement income 117

Annuities 125

Trusts 129
    What is a Trust? 129
    Setting up a Trust 130
    The Trust Deed 130
    Discretionary Trusts 130
    Testamentary Trusts 134

Estate planning 137
    Estate planning paperwork 137

Setting up a Will 139
    What is a Will? 139
    Executors 142
    Powers of attorney 142
    Common questions about Wills 144

More about investments 147
    Why are managed funds widely used? 147
    Superannuation 148
    Insurance 151

Index 154

Introduction

"The secret of getting ahead is getting started."
— Mark Twain

The journey begins

Money.

Money is one thing that evokes such a mixture of emotions and feelings, particularly for Max. It's the root cause of his stress and it doesn't have to be so!

Max is a good man who is married to an even better woman, Lucy. He is an everyday Australian who works hard and does his best in life. Today, he and Lucy are on the road, heading out of Perth to visit a country town for the weekend.

By rights, he should be feeling relaxed and positive on his short getaway with his wife. But he isn't. He is stressed. Stressed about money. He is worried about their future. He realises in his heart of hearts that something should change but he doesn't really know how. He feels like things aren't going his way. Being in tune with what her husband is experiencing, Lucy feels his stress and would also love to find a way to experience less stress about money.

The reality is that they aren't alone. Almost everyone wants money and many experience stress that's related to it. Many people also have an unhealthy relationship or poor habits with their money.

Max and Lucy did not realise that they weren't just going on a weekend away, but also a journey of discovery. They would learn the basic tools to create wealth, to challenge their mindsets to be helpful rather than hindering, and to arm them with more knowledge so that they could be more at peace about money. It couldn't have come at a better time for them.

This is a story to educate, empower and inspire you to a better future, just like Max and Lucy.

Whilst driving, Max reaches for the radio and puts on some music. It isn't long before his mind is awash with thoughts, spinning like a tumble dryer. His attempts to relax are in vain. The stress hasn't dissipated and he asks the question in his head repeatedly – how can I do something? They arrive at their destination, his mind still far away from the present.

They are staying with their friends, Jo and Darcy, and are welcomed with a warm exchange of greetings. Max notices another man emerge from the front door with a happy, peaceful look in his eyes and the look of wisdom and knowledge etched into the character lines of his face. Somehow, Max felt that this man, whoever he was, had something to share and he was curious to explore what it could be. Jo and Darcy introduced him as Uncle Alfred, who would also be staying for the weekend.

Lucy and Max unloaded their luggage and settled in for morning tea with their friends. After a couple of minutes of conversation, Max's curiosity surfaced and he started chatting with Uncle Alfred. Amidst the conversation, Uncle Alfred made a rather accurate observation, saying: "Max, it looks to me as if you are a little stressed. Forgive me for being forward, but is there anything in particular that's causing you stress? I'm asking in case it's something I can help you with."

"Too many thoughts are buzzing around in my mind like a swarm of locusts – first world problems!" Max responded, not entirely sure if he was willing to open up.

"Anything that you would like to talk about?" Uncle Alfred probed.

At this moment, Lucy, being the intuitive person that she was and deft with social graces, sensed the value of a deeper conversation, placed a supportive hand on her husband's thigh and looked at him softly as if asking him to share.

"It's a little embarrassing to admit," Max started, hesitating momentarily and feeling anxious about revealing what was stressing him.

After all, he was brought up in an Australian home where it wasn't common to talk about feelings, so it seemed unusual to him. Jo and Darcy, sensing the energy in the room and potential need for some privacy, announced that they were going out to give the dog a short walk on the property. Max continued when the door closed behind them.

"But I would like to talk about it," he continued. "I'll be honest – for some reason, I feel that you might actually be able to help. The thing is, I'm feeling stressed about money. I'm struggling to keep up, despite earning a good income. I'm not getting ahead and I'm worried about mine and Lucy's future. My wife is such a beautiful person and I am really lucky to be with her, and it stresses me to think that we're not moving ahead financially."

Uncle Alfred beamed with joy, leaving Max and Lucy puzzled by his reaction. You see, Uncle Alfred was the wisest of uncles and happened to be particularly knowledgeable about money. Some had even referred to him as a wise sage.

He realised that Max and Lucy were about to join him on a journey of discovery about money that would benefit them forever.

"If there is one thing I know a lot about, it's money. I have so much to share with you and I invite you both to talk with me over the course of the weekend at some length – in between other activities, of course – and to come with me on a journey of discovery about money," Uncle Alfred explained.

Max and Lucy immediately saw genuine wisdom in Uncle Alfred's face and realised that they were about to be blessed with knowledge. Max suddenly felt a surge of interest and excited anticipation, while Lucy was happy to know that this would likely help her husband feel more at peace.

Jo and Darcy returned to see noticeably brighter looks on their friends' faces. Uncle Alfred and Max explained to their friends what they had briefly discussed with considerable enthusiasm on the part of Max. Jo and Darcy immediately saw the importance of this for their good friends and set about logistically organising the weekend so that they could have a good mixture of time socialising together and time for discussions with Uncle Alfred.

Uncle Alfred suggested that they break up various areas he thought would be beneficial into lessons and have each one build on the other. Max and Lucy had a feeling that their life was about to change positively, which felt terrific.

And so, it began.

Chapter One

Being mindful with money

Lesson One: Your money psychology and money habits

How you think about money and your day-to-day money habits are important.

Your current beliefs may not be serving you as well as you hope. It is time to challenge those and stop to think about what your current attitude to money is like. Reflect on this: is it helping you? If it isn't, commit to making a change here and now. Max and Lucy were on the edge of their seats, listening intently to every word.

Ultimately, what does money give you? Money is a means to an end, a vehicle to experience life. We must balance living life now and building for tomorrow. These thoughts are here to challenge you, to inspire you, to urge you to act in a manner that will serve **your** best interests, and to provide you with some basic tools to take charge of your own journey.

Personally, I will derive a great deal of satisfaction from the fact that information that I have passed on, which has been acted on by you, has helped you get ahead and experience better life outcomes.

Do you currently:

- ◆ Associate having a lot of money, or those that do, with being a bad person?
- ◆ Do you have insufficient savings to your name and personal credit owing (e.g. outstanding credit cards, personal loans)?
- ◆ Are you directing any money towards investments?
- ◆ Do you know that you have habits that don't serve you in accumulating wealth?

If you answered yes to one or all of these, then, firstly, understand that many are in the same boat, so be kind to yourself and recognise that this doesn't help you. Secondly, it's time to make changes, re-decide, and shift the mindset.

"Yes, that's us!" exclaimed Max. "We don't have any savings to our name, two credit cards that forever have a balance, and we never seem to have any money even though I know that our family income is quite good."

"It's time to make a decision to change that right now!" Uncle Alfred said with considerable passion, looking directly at Max and Lucy.

"I'm committed to change. I want something better for Lucy and I!" Max declared with steely resolve. The positive energy in the room was nothing short of inspiring.

A word on personal credit:

As alluded to already, having credit card debts, personal loans, and loans used for lifestyle purposes do not help you get ahead financially. Having these in your situation is like a sprinter having a hamstring strain and then attempting to sprint at their best – it doesn't work very well! So, if this is you, I challenge you to make a decision now to change it. If you have always had this kind of debt in your situation, realise that your habits must change. If your credit cards have always had an amount owing, maybe you should get rid of them altogether and operate without them.

You can do it!

The money manifesto:

In our society, which is largely a well-educated one, it is my observation that many people do not manage their money well, which works against them. I want something better for you than this. Make a decision right now to commit to doing the right things in order to build wealth – your future depends on it. Change this reality for you and your family. Below is my money manifesto, which will ultimately help you:

1) Live within your means. Spend less on your lifestyle than you earn. It's a basic idea, but say it to yourself again and make it a concept that is forever in your mind. If you are doing something different to this, change! Many people may already know this, but you need to **LIVE it**!

2) As in the famous and well-worn book, *The Richest Man in Babylon*, part of your income is yours to keep. That is, part of your income should always be put aside for savings and investments. Do this as a **starting point**, not as an afterthought. This is a mindset – a habit – and it will ultimately assist you in building wealth.

3) Decide what percentage of your salary you wish to save and invest, then live off the rest.

4) Consider using automated savings strategies to effectively save and invest your money. That is, use strategies that happen in the background that you don't have to think about too much and they'll work in your favour. For example, simply paying an extra $1,000 per month off your mortgage is one valid method to build a better position, as is starting an investment plan with automatic regular payments going into it. The reason for this is that no one is 100% efficient with money. Therefore, automating an outcome helps.

5) If you do not have the money to buy something discretionary, then don't buy it. Wait until you do. Good money management involves an element of discipline.

6) Keep a cash reserve in your situation on an ongoing basis so that, if the unexpected crops up, you have cash available to use in this situation.

7) Think about debt carefully. Whenever you use debt or borrowed money to buy an asset as an investment,

there is more risk associated with the investment than if you didn't. That doesn't mean that borrowing to invest should not be done. Just realise the risk involved and make sure that you are comfortable to undertake this. Beware of excessive borrowing because, in almost every economic downturn, those that have too much debt can get caught out where asset prices reduce significantly.

8) Personal debt has no place in your situation, nor does it help you financially. Unless it's absolutely necessary, borrow money only for purchasing assets that may rise in value. That means that the **only** credit card balance that works is a **zero** balance each month. If you struggle to do this, then do yourself a favour right now – get out the scissors and cut it (or them!) up now and get rid of your credit cards completely.

9) Whenever you receive a pay rise, decide what percentage of this raise you wish to save and invest and what percentage you wish to use for adding to your lifestyle. For example, you may choose for 30% of a pay rise to be saved or invested. Once you have made this decision, make it happen in an automated way and stick to it. The relative value of doing this throughout your career can make a substantial difference to your position.

10) Start investing early and give yourself the longest period of time possible in order to build assets and build a passive income.

11) Protect yourself with quality insurances.
12) Improve yourself continually over time to increase your income-earning capacity.

Uncle Alfred paused to look at Max and Lucy, checking if what he had said was sinking in.

"Great!" exclaimed Max with palpable excitement. "So, live within your means; pay yourself first; continually save a percentage of your salary, ideally with automated savings; have a cash reserve; see that some of your pay rise gets saved and invested; invest over a long period of time; protect yourself with insurance and do what you can to increase your income." Max mentally ticked each point off, ensuring that they were etched into his mind. Lucy sat beside Max, also soaking in the information with interest.

Making behavioural change:

Take action!! There are people who know that they are doing things in their lives that are not helping them, yet they continue to do so. Such things as not eating enough vegetables and fruit in a diet, when this is known to be part of a healthy lifestyle. Why is that?

We need to dig deeper psychologically to make lasting changes. We need to love ourselves and be kind to ourselves so that we are more likely to take actions that aid us and not hinder us. What is important is making a behavioural change towards the right behaviour. As Tony Robbins says, get in touch with the pain points in your situation. Understand and write down what **pain** it's causing you if you are not eating your vegetables and what **pleasure** will result from changing this behaviour.[1] The analogy here is that your vegetables are your money habits.

So, do this for your money habits if you know in your heart of hearts that they are not serving you well. The point is to get in touch with some strong emotional drivers that will be more effective in helping you shift your behaviour. Then, set about making small incremental steps in the right direction, which builds positive momentum. In short, take action!

A further tool to help build positive psychology and momentum towards meaningful progress is a ritual board – a concept that Paul Taylor introduced.[2] The manner in which Paul Taylor uses this is in having little habits that work towards a healthy lifestyle. By ticking them off, you create positive feedback. You can use this same idea and modify the rituals to apply it specifically to creating and using new habits that work towards building a better life, including money habits. You might change this ritual board depending on what you are working towards at any given time. This is a tool aimed at getting you to change to a better pattern of habits and to stick with it. Whatever works for you!

---

[1] *Awaken the Giant Within*, By Anthony Robbins.
[2] https://vimeo.com/84756930 **Paul Taylor; Ritual Board**

Ritual	Mon	Tues	Wed	Thur	Fri	Sat	Sun
Being aware of what I've spent							
Keep to my life expenditure plan							
Exercise							
Get 7 hours or more of sleep							
Healthy eating							
My savings/ investments allocated							
Spending quality time with my family							
Fun/downtime							
Walk the dog							
Learn the piano							
Do home chores							

"Uncle Alfred, I have a question," Lucy queried. "I think we need to do something to get a better idea of living within our means first and to actually be able to build a cash reserve. How do we go about that? And what is a life expenditure plan that you have in your ritual board example?"

"Great questions Lucy! If you realise that you need a better handle on what you currently spend in your life and how to get to a balanced version of spending less than you earn, that is where a life expenditure plan comes in. Some people call it a budget, but life expenditure plan is easier to digest and it is all about what you earmark for expenditure for your lifestyle.[3] So, firstly, invest some time into getting an idea about what you are currently spending in your life. There are templates available that help you get the full picture. These can be helpful since some expenses you only pay for every now and again, such as twice a year. Then, consider whether the life expenditure plan requires any adjustments. Work out a reasonable level of life spending that enables some percentage of savings to take place. If you are changing habits, you may want to track your life expenditure plan for at least a while to ensure that you stay on track," Uncle Alfred explained.

---

[3] A template for a life expenditure plan is included in the Bonus chapter.

Chapter One
Summary Learning Points:

- Check that your relationship with money is one that helps you instead of hinders you and change it if necessary.
- Personal credit is like a strained hamstring for a sprinter – not useful!
- Adopt the money manifesto, which includes:
  - Spend less on your lifestyle than you earn.
  - Part of your income should always be put aside for savings and investment. Do this as a **starting point**, not as an afterthought.
  - Decide what percentage of your salary you wish to save and invest, then live off the rest.
  - Consider using automated savings strategies to effectively save and invest your money.
  - Keep a cash reserve or contingency fund on an ongoing basis.
  - Think about debt carefully and use it carefully.
  - Use a proportion of each pay rise to add further funds to savings and investments.
  - Start investing as early as you can and give yourself as much time as possible.

- ▶ Improve yourself and your income-earning capacity.
- ▶ Protect yourself with quality insurances.
- ◆ Make behavioural changes where you realise it is needed. Two tools to help increase effectiveness include:
  - ▶ Getting in touch with what **pain** it's causing you by continuing your current ineffective habits, and what **pleasure** will result from changing the behaviour.
  - ▶ Use a ritual board with small habits recorded to build meaningful progress and positive psychology around the change.
- ◆ Make a lifestyle expenditure plan to help identify what amount beyond the cost of living can be saved and invested.

Chapter Two

Setting the path

Lesson Two: Goal setting

Having come back from a bush walk, Uncle Alfred, Max and Lucy sat down again for the second lesson.

In thinking about your life and growing your wealth, goal setting and effectively working towards them is very important. The focus here will mainly be on financial goal setting. However, I encourage you to set goals for any aspect of your life and come back to review them, re-focus and keep yourself accountable to them.

Let's pause to think for a moment: why set goals and why is it valuable?

- Goals help you focus. Once you have set and written down a goal, it helps keep your mind on the target.
- Having goals allows you to measure your progress. So, quantifying your goals is important to do and provides a clear measuring point, enabling you to see your progress and ask yourself if you are on the right track.

- Having goals and focussing your mind on them helps avoid distractions and provides a form of mental boundary.
- Having goals helps overcome procrastination by making yourself accountable to finish the task or reach the objective, which can help galvanise you into action.
- Goal setting can provide you with motivation and help drive your momentum. That concrete end point gives you something to focus your energies towards.

The well-known author, Stephen Covey, has been quoted widely as saying "begin with the end in mind", which is exactly what goal setting is all about. If you understand where you are heading, it can help you in determining the most effective course of action to get there, including galvanising your energies in the right direction.

"I must admit, I've never really written down any goals. I have occasionally worked towards something specific, but mostly, I've just bumbled along," shared Max. Lucy nodded beside him.

"Let me tell you a story. One day, when I was a young child, I loved riding my bike but still had to use training wheels. I decided on a goal and announced it to my parents that, by the end of the day, I'd ride my bike without training wheels. This was my goal, and I spent hours out on the driveway practising and practising. I clearly wasn't the most natural bike rider, but setting the goal gave me the focus I needed and, after five hours of trying, I succeeded," Uncle Alfred shared.

"Come to think of it," Max said. "I did do the Perth City to Surf 12km run last year for the very first time. When I decided to do it, I set about training and running three times a week so that I had the best chance of finishing in reasonable shape. It just hit me that this is an example of a goal, though non-financial. It was really effective in galvanising action at the time and it was a great experience. I felt proud of myself because I'd never run that far before."

Max had just made a psychological link and realised the relevance of goal setting.

Financial goal setting requires you to use your imagination to understand more about what you wish to achieve. Given that it's not always apparent straight away, this is potentially where talking to a professional will come in helpful in exploring the topic and helping you uncover more of what you aspire for. When you ask yourself what you would like to achieve financially, don't feel concerned if the picture is a little cloudy at first.

It can also help to think about aspects of your financial life such as when you would like to repay your mortgage by, accumulating enough wealth to provide a passive income that could replace your cost of living, having funds available to take overseas holidays, or possibly helping the kids out in the future with their first home.

When setting goals, the S.M.A.R.T. format is a well-known and effective way to go about it. This is an acronym that means:

S: Specific: a goal that is specific in nature will have a far greater chance of being accomplished. For example, a specific goal might be to have $10,000 as a cash reserve, not just to have a cash reserve which is a more general statement.

M: Measurable: quantify your goal. This helps to track your progress towards the goal and will enable you to understand when you have reached it.

A: Attainable: set a goal that is attainable to reach. Goals can be a stretch but, ultimately, you want the process to have you in a positive mental state and energise you towards it. Therefore, make it attainable. If you reach it sooner than you think, you can always set another larger goal.

R: Realistic: the goal should be something you are willing and able to work towards. So, make it realistic. It should be something that stretches and motivates, within the realms of realism.

T: Timing or time-based: there should be a time period associated with achieving your goal because this sets the clock ticking, creates a sense of urgency and helps make the goal more specific.

"My financial planner uses the following format to help articulate financial goals, which also incorporates an additional concept: getting you to imagine the feeling or emotion you will have when that goal is achieved. This is done to further motivate and inspire," added Uncle Alfred.

Goal Description:

Goal Target date:

....

Two or three words describing feelings and thoughts when achieved:

"Hang on a second, you have a financial planner even though you know so much? Why?" asked Max.

"That is an excellent question," Uncle Alfred said. "For me, the key reason is accountability. I do have a deep understanding of money and have studied finance and financial planning myself. However, I'm not perfect and my planner is my financial coach, like a sporting coach, challenging me to get more out of myself and my finances."

An example goal using this format might be:

Have a cash reserve of $20,000 accumulated in 12 months' time by 1 July 2018. Two or three words describing the feeling when achieved are: greater security, accomplishment, and pride.

So, what else can be done to enhance the effectiveness of goal setting and reaching your goals?

1) Break down your goals into smaller, bite-sized actions that will lead you to the objective, then **take action**!
2) Track your progress and keep yourself accountable. Be aware that your goals may change over time, and that is okay. So, the process of reviewing this, checking that you're on track and adjusting what you are doing to be most effective are all important.

In order to break your goals down into smaller steps, you can use the following:

GOAL (include date for achieving this):

What steps must I take in order to accomplish my goal? (these can be effectively smaller action items that will lead to the main objective)

A quality, trusted adviser can coach you in the right direction and keep you accountable to what YOU want to achieve.

So, goal setting and keeping yourself on track are important in building wealth. Just as setting a goal jump-started Max into action for the City to Surf 12km run, it can do so for your money, too.

"There is some more colour to add to this lesson," Uncle Alfred continued. "That is, enjoy the journey and really enjoy the process of working towards whatever it is that you set out to do with an attitude of being grateful for what you have. This attitude of gratitude has psychological links with people being happier, so, why not? Enjoying the journey is key, as is noticing the feeling of positive momentum and meaningful progress. Sometimes, this brings greater happiness than the goal itself, so celebrate your momentum and progress along the way. This is where having rituals (such as a version of the ritual board) or ongoing habits can drive the forward momentum towards what you are seeking to achieve."

Lucy, as the intuitive astute type of person she is, realised that Uncle Alfred's words had some real depth and meaning.

Chapter Two
Summary Learning Points:

- Goal setting helps galvanise you into action.
- Financial goal setting may be challenging to quantify initially. Discussing this with your partner and potentially a professional adviser and considering various areas of your financial life can help, such as:
  - When do you wish to repay your mortgage by?
  - Building wealth and your long-term income objectives.
  - Setting goals for overseas travel expenditure.
  - Do you wish to help your children financially in the future?
- Set goals with the S.M.A.R.T. methodology to increase effectiveness.
- Once you have set goals, break them down into smaller action items so that you have an action plan to help you achieve each goal. Then, take action!!
- Enjoy the journey on the path to your financial goals and maintain a positive demeanour with an attitude of gratitude. Notice your meaningful progress along the way and celebrate forward momentum.

Chapter Three

Building wealth

LESSON THREE: Reaching financial security and financial freedom

The lottery is not the answer. Let me repeat that – the lottery is not the answer!! The number of lottery winners who end up bankrupt is startling.

It's frightening to think how many people have this as their financial plan. Regardless of the level of income and assets you have, you must still maintain good money-management habits (**Lesson One**).

With reaching financial security and freedom, start on the track as soon as you can and head towards it as consistently as you can. If you are struggling to see the way forward, seek help!

What does financial security and financial freedom mean to you? It is a broad term that, ultimately, means different things to different people. What would you be doing with your life and would your lifestyle be any different if you reached this point?

In reaching financial outcomes, pay attention to visualising and thinking about what your **lifestyle** would look like. What would you be doing with your time? How would you most like to use your time? There is absolutely no point in having a truck load of money and being bored if you have retired and not set enough for yourself to do in your post-retirement life. It's highly relevant to be considering this, but it is often forgotten. So, make sure that you think about this clearly and well ahead of time. For some, part of the answer here could be continuing to work even when financial resources are plentiful, just for the mental and social stimulation it provides.

How we define **financial security** is having sufficient resources so that the income from those investments can provide for the fundamentals or **basics** in your life. You may still need to or wish to work at this point to have some of the nice-to-have elements in your lifestyle, with the basics already covered by investments.

Here is an example based on an Australian household. *Note: this is an example only and everyone's requirements and situation is slightly different.* Jack and Alice consider the following to be their basics of living each month:

Home mortgage	$2,015
Utilities and rates	309
Insurances	380
Mobile phones and internet	230
Food	480
Transport basics	300
Bought lunches	320
Total per month	**$4,034**

Consider the above basics of living for Jack and Alice. If they had their mortgage repaid, how would this change the monthly amount?

Financial freedom is about having enough income generated from investments to provide all requirements for your lifestyle. Exactly what that number is depends on your lifestyle expectations and the level of income that meets this definition for you.

For Jack and Alice, this is what they consider to be their total cost of living each month:

Home mortgage	$2,015
Utilities	$309
Insurances	$380
Transport	$540
Food including entertainment	$1,230
Education	$1,470
Medical	$92
Personal including gifts and clothing	$326
Holidays	$500
Incidentals	$93
Total per month	**$6,955**

At its core, financial security and financial freedom are about having sufficient money available to provide you with choices and flexibility. This is where the real power lies – in having life choices and flexibility and working because you want to, not because you must. Therefore, we define wealth as providing a passive income that supports your lifestyle – not just how big your assets are, but rather the income that flows from these assets that will provide you with **real** flexibility.

In most cases, people's requirements often grow once they get close to attaining a goal. This is not a bad thing if it doesn't stop you from enjoying some of your successes. Some can struggle psychologically to feel financially secure even if they reach an objective that they, themselves, have set because they keep moving the threshold higher. This is something to be careful of. Whilst it is important to be conservative and have more than you require, it is also important to relax and enjoy the fruits of your toil within the bounds of sound money-management habits.

Lucy and Max sat intently, soaking up the information that they had learned and eager to learn more. Having had a break, they settled in to hear the next lesson.

Lesson Four: Effectively building wealth

How do you build wealth?
Broadly and simply, there are a couple of ways to do this:

1) Use some of your income and financial resources over time to buy financial assets that can grow in value and provide income. This may or may not involve borrowing, such as buying a house with a mortgage and paying it off over time.
2) Create something of value that wasn't there before, such as building a business.

Building a business or investing in a business to grow it, can and have been effective ways to build wealth. However, be aware that many businesses may not succeed, so tread with caution. The purpose of these lessons is to focus on the first of these ways of building wealth. We will come back to comment broadly on building a business later.

Wealth is built by effectively directing some of your income towards savings and investments that can grow in value over time. Be clear that what we are talking about here is long-term wealth creation. You should avoid get-rich-quick schemes and, at the very least, be extremely sceptical about them. So, this starts with getting a handle on your lifestyle expenditure and efficiently directing some of your money towards investments. As mentioned earlier, a lifestyle expenditure plan will give you an indication of how much you have in surplus to direct towards investments. Of course, remember that there may be the need to alter your plan to bring down expenditure to increase capacity for investment.

Accelerating wealth creation:

"So, Uncle Alfred, how do we go about accelerating the process of building wealth?" Lucy asked.

"Accelerating your accumulation of wealth starts with looking at the various inputs to the process and enhancing those," Uncle Alfred responded. "We will now talk about each of them in turn."

1) Invest in yourself and raise your income-earning capacity.

Warren Buffett[4] has been known to say that the best investment you can make is in yourself. I believe this is true. Ask yourself how you can be the most valuable version of yourself. What does this mean that you should do to work towards it? How can you be of most value to society?

Linked with these questions is the idea of building your income-earning capacity – working on continuous improvements to increase your income. Investing in yourself and building your income-earning capacity is one important aspect to accelerating wealth.

---

[4] https://en.wikipedia.org/wiki/Warren_Buffett **Warren Buffett is one of the most famous and successful investors of all time, from the USA.**

2) Consider tax and fees.

What really matters when investing is the **after** tax and **after** fee return. Paying more tax than you should can have a significant and detrimental impact on long-term wealth creation. So, determine the most tax-efficient manner for investments for you. This is an area where seeking good advice can assist in evaluating strategies that work towards your objectives and considering the amount of risk that you are comfortable with.

Therefore, invest your tax effectively within the rules and look at the total return after fees to do what you can to maximise this.

3) Being more efficient with saving and investing.

If you can effectively invest 30% of your income instead of 10% over a long period of time, it will make a substantial difference to your wealth creation. To illustrate the difference this can make, here is a case study:

> Derek and Janice are friends and commit to investing a percentage of their income in a managed portfolio over 20 years. As it happens, they both work in the same company and earn the same income of $200,000 per annum. Derek saves and invests 10% of his income, whilst Janice is committed to a higher level of savings of 30%. Both use the same index portfolio, which provides an average of 8% rate of return over time.

With the only difference in their experience being the percentage that they commit to investing, what do you think the different might be after 20 years? In today's dollar terms, Janice has over **$1 million** more in her portfolio than in Derek's portfolio. That is massive!! *Note: there are assumptions here on the rate of return achieved and be aware that the reality will never be exactly as the calculation has shown.* Investments rarely provide an 8% return each year, instead you might get something like 10% one year, 3% the next, -2% one year and 14% the next. Regardless of this fact, the illustrated point remains valid and pronounced. That is, being more efficient with your saving over a long period is highly likely to produce a far better outcome for you.

Derek		Janice	
$200,000 income		$200,000 income	
10% of income:	$20,000/yr	30% of income:	$60,000/yr
8% return		8% return	
Time frame:	20 years	Time frame:	20 years
Future value:	$915,239	Future value:	$2,745,718
Present value:	$506,746	Present value:	$1,520,237
Difference (FV):		$1,830,479	
Difference (PV):		$1,013,491	

Assumptions used in the calculation:
1. The amount invested is done so every year.
2. The return on portfolio is 8%.
3. The time frame is 20 years.
4. The starting balance is 0.
5. Factor to discount to present value = 1.806111, which assumes 3% inflation over 20 years.

"Wow! That's huge!" Max exclaimed with amazement.

4) Be consistent.

Some people start investing with several of the other factors listed above very well weighted in their favour. But then they stop – they don't continue to invest and don't keep adding to the honey pot. Being consistent and investing regularly can also help in smoothing out returns in volatile markets. It can help to psychologically think of this as "another bill" as most people are good at making sure they keep up with their bills.

5) Start early.

The longer you have to invest, the easier it is to generate wealth. It would be ideal if you were to start your career and commence investing for long-term wealth generation from the start. But if this isn't where you are up to in life right now, don't worry – there is no time like the present.

6) Continue with sound money management.

As mentioned in Lesson One, continue with the sound principles of money management – the money manifesto – over the long term, which will serve you well.

7) Clear and well-thought-out analysis.

Clearly, evaluating investment options and performing a balanced investigation on an investment or investments is important. Our psychology is an important factor. At various times where the economy is booming, investments are providing strong returns and the mood of the day is optimistic, it can be that we build overly optimistic assumptions or develop temporary amnesia and forget that investments can go **up** and **also down**. Conversely, in a negative market environment, people will tend to be more cautious and potentially overly pessimistic. The trick is to consider the investment or investments with a balanced mind, having done sound research. Look at the possible advantages, disadvantages and risks and challenge your thinking, considering if you have a particular bias in your thinking, which is often the case. This can be a great point to seek assistance for if you feel you wish to.

Checklist of questions to ask yourself to help in making good financial decisions:

Often when we are looking at a financial decision, emotion (including excitement) can be a contributing factor. And whilst this can be a good thing, it is important to ensure that a balance of relevant and prudent factors is considered.

Here is a checklist of questions to ask yourself with any investment:

1) Relevant facts:

- Do the potential financial outcomes assist me in working towards my own financial goals?
- What are the costs that are associated with this investment?
- What about the people involved in this investment – are they of sound character, reputable and to be relied upon?
- Do I have all relevant information to make a good decision? Do I need to seek specialist advice to help me in doing so?
- How long am I willing to hold this investment? Am I willing to hold it long enough to see a gain that may take time to eventuate?

2) Upside potential:

- What are the likely financial outcomes? What can I reasonably expect out of this?

- Do the economic conditions of the current time and in the next five years (and beyond) support this investment, giving a good long-term return?

3) Downsides and risks:

- What are the downsides and risks that I need to consider? What is the worst-case scenario?
- Am I comfortable with the level of borrowing associated with this investment? Am I comfortable that I am not taking on too much gearing? *Remember: the more you borrow, the higher the risk.*
- Have I got a contingency buffer factored in? *Note: contingency buffers are a good idea.*

4) Deciding

- What does my gut tell me? What is my gut feeling?
- Specifically, why is it a good idea that I invest in this particular asset or assets now?
- What are the psychological and emotional factors relevant to this investment for me? Am I giving them the right amount of weight, too much, or too little?

Having gone through the checklist, actively decide if it is something that you wish to pursue or not.

Lucy and Max both absorbed this information intently, taking notes as they went.

Being contrarian in your thinking:

Warren Buffett has famously said "be greedy **ONLY** when others are fearful and fearful when others are greedy." This quickly sums up what it means to be contrarian – to think and act in a way that is different to the masses. The reality is that the biggest opportunities come after a market downturn. This is, again, a time for clear analysis to determine investments that are worth buying in this time period. For example, if you bought a selection of **exceptional** companies following the global financial crisis when the entire market was undervalued and held them for long enough, you would have made a very good return indeed.

Again, doing your homework and having cash available to take advantage of such situations is critical. The point here is recognising the time periods when there are bigger opportunities available than there usually are, and finding a way to act on them.

"So, who is Warren Buffett? And are you talking about a market downturn in regards to investment markets such as shares?" Max queried.

"Yes, that's what I meant," Uncle Alfred said. "Warren Buffett is one of the most well-known and successful investors of all time and lives in America. He has written and provided a lot of guidance over the years aimed at helping others."

"Adding to what I've just said," he continued. "Let me take an example company from the global financial crisis. Now, let me be clear – I'm not saying that you should invest in just one company, nor am I saying that this is the best company around, but it illustrates my point about bigger opportunities being available after a downturn. Wesfarmers is an Australian company that, during the global financial crisis, got down to about $15 per share and was trading at double this two to three years later. So, in this window of time, there was a real opportunity with the right companies. Wesfarmers did, indeed, have its challenges at the time, so there was still a risk with this investment that it wouldn't work out."

"Okay, that makes sense then," Max said.

When investing, construct a high-quality investment portfolio:

Another factor that has a clear bearing on the creation of wealth is the **actual** return that your investments provide over time. Therefore, when investing, construct a portfolio of very high-quality assets.

Use of debt:

Using borrowed funds to invest can potentially accelerate wealth creation, but not always. Typically, it is something that almost all of us do in buying a home: getting a mortgage to help pay for it with borrowed funds. However, a **strong word of warning: debt can also magnify losses; when debt is involved, take care**. Remember that nearly all downturns or recessions are because of too much debt in the system. So, use debt to your advantage **if** you are comfortable in doing so, but not too heavily or beware of the possible consequences. The way you can counter the risks of borrowing is to not borrow too heavily. Alternatively, you can invest in some managed funds which uses gearing internally as opposed to borrowing funds yourself. Sound and prudent advice on this topic is strongly recommended because, if done incorrectly, it has the potential to ruin your financial wealth creation entirely (worst-case scenario).

Review your investments and progress:

Reviewing your investments periodically can also help accelerate your wealth because, at certain points (not always), you may realise that action should be taken to lock in strong returns or to safeguard your portfolio. The act of reviewing and making clear and prudent decisions is a great idea. For example, if you have bought an investment property with borrowing attached to it and, over the last five years, it has substantially risen in value – much higher than the average

5% to 6% capital growth on property that you may see over a longer term – then it may be worthwhile considering if you should realise this gain.

Of course, tax and costs must be considered and it may be that you decide to keep it, but it is worth carefully reviewing where you have experienced a return on your investment(s) that is much higher or lower than the long-term average returns expected. Often, when investments have gained much more than is normally anticipated, this super-charged growth is unlikely to continue.

Lesson Five: Building wealth through a business

If you are partial to reading the rich-list publications, you may notice that there is a high proportion of people who have a business or have an interest in a business that has generated a sizeable amount of wealth for them and is the key reason that they are on such lists. For the ultra-wealthy, it is almost always part of the picture.

Building a business is a valid and potentially inspiring pursuit, but it does not guarantee success or wealth. In fact, the reality is that most business owners find it difficult to be successful. So, if you are considering this in your situation, think carefully about the opportunity and the cost of what you would otherwise earn as an employee or consultant. Be honest with yourself in relation to if you want to keep that lifestyle separation between work and your home life, which is something many business owners struggle to do given they are so invested.

Here are some things for you to think about if this is something that you aspire to do:

1) Do your homework. Research the business you are creating or buying and ask yourself lots of high-quality questions. Why is this going to work? What are the risks? How am I going to go about this? How am I going to be different from other competitors? Is there

a sufficient market opportunity present? Make sure that you construct a useable business plan. Some business plans can be vast in length and sit in the office drawer, not being referred to until the end of the financial year. Clearly, this is not useful enough. So, it is far better to have a short, to the point, clear and concise business plan that hits the key elements, that you look at regularly, and can track and work towards.

2) It is a good idea to construct conservative cash flow projections for your business. Your accountant can assist you with this. What type of revenues and costs are you anticipating?

3) Seek advice from your accountant on your business and the most appropriate structure to be used.

4) Speak to other people in similar businesses to see what insight you can get from them.

5) Visit the small business development centre or state government business resources centre where you live.

6) Read an excellent business book, *The E-Myth Revisited* by Michael Gerber.

7) Ensure that you have finances and funding for the business sorted out, including having sufficient working capital in place, which is an important element in any business. Build contingencies into your models.

8) Ask yourself why you want to do this, what your business purpose is, and if it is likely to achieve the financial, lifestyle and other objectives that you have.

9) When you get started, track your progress regularly and know what is happening in your business so that you can adapt as, and where, necessary.

10) Assuming that you have started a business and are making good money, be clear to use profits in the most effective way possible. At the end of the day, make sure that the business profits paid to you are effectively being invested to grow your wealth passively. In other words, **make your business success count for your personal wealth creation**.

Chapter Three

Summary Learning Points:

- Financial security and financial freedom can be considered as two different levels on the road to accumulating wealth, with security enabling passive income to meet basic costs of living, and freedom enabling passive income to meet the full cost of living.

- Consider your lifestyle and what you would do with your time if you have sufficient resources. This is a key point; it is not just about having enough money but also about creating a lifestyle for yourself that sees you fulfilled, enriched and living.

- Building wealth happens through:
  - Effectively directing income to savings and investments over time.
  - Creating something of value, such as a business.

- The process of building wealth can be accelerated by:
  - Investing in yourself and improving your income-earning capacity.
  - Investing in the most tax-efficient manner with a sound net return.
  - Saving and investing a higher proportion of your income.

- ▶ Consistently and regularly investing.
- ▶ Continue with sound money management.
- ▶ Conduct sound analysis.
- ▶ Buy high-quality investments.
- ▶ Thinking differently than the crowd.
- ▶ Use of debt (with care).
- ▶ Reviewing investments and progress periodically.

◆ Building wealth through a business is something that can work for you, though there are many cases of business failure and struggle.

◆ Care and homework is required for investing in a business to ensure that you are doing it for the right reasons. Have a plan, track your progress and adapt and refine as you go.

Chapter Four

Deep dive into investing

Lesson Six: More about investing

At this point in their weekend away, having had some great lessons coupled with some relaxing down time, both Max and Lucy were feeling positively energised. Lucy was particularly keen to learn more about investing. So, Uncle Alfred continued.

Remember the levers you can pull to accelerate wealth? As a reminder, they are:

- Invest in yourself and your income earning capacity.
- Invest tax and fees effectively.
- Improve your rate of savings and directing resources to investments.
- Be consistent and start as early as you can.
- Adopt clear analysis and thinking.
- Have high-quality investments.

- Think differently to the masses.
- Review your progress.
- For some, not all, **careful** use of debt.

When investing, people often make the mistake of not thinking long term. Investing is a long-term game and the power of compound returns really starts to show the longer you have your investment. So, forget about "making a motza" in a couple of years, which will often lead people to high-risk investments without sufficient proven payoffs and a real risk of failure. Instead, focus on long-term wealth creation. The one caveat to this is if you invest after a big market downturn, where it is possible to make stronger returns but without guarantee.

Consider this story illustrating the power of long-term compound returns:

> James and Jennifer are brother and sister. They both understand that they should invest some of their money in order to build wealth over time, but their approach differs and Jennifer doesn't get around to doing anything about it for some time. James starts early – from the start of his career – and commits to an ultra-long-term and consistent regular savings plan. Jennifer adopts an identical approach, starting her regular investments at age 40.

Both start with a capital value of **$5,000** and invest **$400** per month into an investment plan. James starts at age 23 and stops at 65 years of age, where Jennifer starts hers at age 40 until age 65. Both portfolios provide an average of 8% per annum compound return. Naturally, the actual rate of return does have a bearing on wealth creation and won't be exactly 8% each year. Instead, the return achieved will be different each year, but would average 8% over time. Therefore, calculations aren't exact but do give an indication of long-term compound returns.

What do you think their final balances are?

For James, his investment is worth **$1,718,831**. What a balance! A sizeable amount which has been built up over time. Who would have thought that it could get to this from $5,000?

For Jennifer, hers is **$385,150**. It's still a fantastic amount of money, but substantially less than James has.

The power of compound returns accelerates as you have more time. The longer you have, the more this can benefit you. Imagine how you can help your kids, grandchildren, or nieces and nephews with this concept!

"Gee, that's such a difference! Lucy and I are looking to start a family soon, so I'm going to remember that for our future kids," Max said with noticeable excitement.

For the purpose of education on various types of investments that we talk about here, there are a few types of investments we are referring to, namely:

- Australian share investments (such as the Commonwealth Bank).
- International share investments (such as Google or Nestle).
- Fixed interest investments, including government bonds.
- Cash.
- Property investments (listed or unlisted).
- Managed funds, which are a vehicle or way in which to invest in a portfolio of investments that can vary to include some or all of the above.

What are managed funds?

A managed fund is an investment portfolio that individual investors can buy into, purchasing **units** rather than shares. An investment manager will monitor and manage the investments in the portfolio, for the benefit of unit holders.

Each managed fund has a specific investment objective, which is usually based around the different asset classes (cash, fixed interest, property, and shares) or a mix of all asset classes. The money you invest is used to buy assets in line with this investment objective.

When you invest in a managed fund, you are allocated a number of units. The value of your units is calculated on a daily basis and changes as the market value of the assets in the fund rises and falls.

"So, managed funds are pooled investments in a large portfolio in which you have unit entitlements in? A type of unit trust, then?" Lucy interjects.

"Yes, that's right Lucy!" affirmed Uncle Alfred.

Lesson Seven: Things to know for constructing an investment portfolio

Care should be taken when constructing a quality investment portfolio to effectively build your wealth. Here are some principles to guide you in thinking about investments. *Note: good advice can assist you in building a portfolio tailored specifically for you so that you don't have to remember it all, but it is useful to understand.*

Understanding risk and the expected outcome:

Risk in the context of investment is the chance that you may lose money on your investments. This is an important consideration and you should **start** with minimising and considering risks when investing.

When constructing a portfolio, it is important to invest in a manner that is consistent with the level of risk that you are comfortable taking. For example, if you are a conservative investor, you should not be borrowing to invest as this is too risky for your comfort. If you have an adviser, they will conduct an assessment through a discussion and questionnaire to help you identify where you are on the risk spectrum. Generally speaking, investments that carry a higher level of risk tend to have the potential to deliver higher returns, such as **growth assets** like shares, property and infrastructure. Those with the potential to deliver lower returns, such as cash and fixed interest, generally carry lower risk levels.

The one caveat to the above relationship is with shares in isolation. The relationship between risk and return when looking solely at a share portfolio is slightly different. That is, it has been shown over time that low-risk, profitable companies tend to have a very similar long-term return outcome as companies that are considered to be high-risk. In this instance, a sound investment philosophy is to opt within a share portfolio for **lower**-risk companies with strong fundamental characteristics.

When thinking of investment returns, a factor that is highly relevant is the potential of a portfolio to have **negative returns** and how you can minimise negative returns in poor market conditions. Of course, negative investment returns **can and do happen** at times and markets go up and down in cycles, which is to be expected. However, minimising your portfolio "drawdown" in these periods is important. For example, if your investment portfolio decreased by 50%, then you would require a subsequent 100% return for the portfolio to return to the break-even point. As the negative return gets larger, the return required to break even grows. The following table illustrates this relationship:

Drawdown:	Gain Required to Break Even:
5%	5%
10%	11%
15%	18%
20%	25%
25%	33%
30%	43%
35%	54%
40%	67%
45%	82%
50%	100%
75%	300%
90%	900%

(**Source:** http://www.arborinvestmentplanner.com/probable-maximum-loss/
http://www.biznews.com/wealth-building/2014/09/30/can-ever-recover-investment-loss-returns-must-make-easy-use-table/)

"If you have a portfolio that is estimated to provide you with a 7% long-term return and a second, alternate portfolio that is estimated to provide you with a 6.8% long-term return with a lower probability of negative returns and expected to have a lower drawdown, which would you choose? Mitigating risk is a key and important aspect with long-term, quality investment portfolios," Uncle Alfred explained.

"Wow, you really do know a lot about investments, Uncle Alfred! I would choose the 6.8% option with a lower risk after what you have said," Max said with energy.

Diversification:

Despite good research and planning, any given asset may not give an outcome as good as you are anticipating. The concept of diversification is commonly referred to as not putting all of your eggs in one basket. That is, have a spread of multiple investments in a portfolio rather than focussing on one investment.

The intention of diversification is to, first and foremost, minimise portfolio risk. Diversification can happen both within an asset class (such as shares) and across the portfolio by having investments in more than one type of asset (such as shares, fixed interest and property rather than just in property).

Although this concept is sound and well-accepted, care must be taken with the implementation to get a sufficient spread of risk without over-diversifying for no additional benefit.

Asset allocation:

The asset allocation of your portfolio – the percentage of funds you have in shares, fixed interest, property, international shares and cash – is an important determinant in the overall return of your portfolio. Some asset classes perform differently in varying economic conditions. So, by having a mix, you can reduce the risk across your portfolio and potentially add to your long-term return. Later in this book, we will briefly describe the typical characteristics of the asset classes for your knowledge and information.

Liquidity:

When investing, the liquidity of your prospective assets should be considered. An asset with high liquidity can be quickly converted into cash, while a direct commercial property may be relatively illiquid, meaning that it could take six months or longer for the asset to be sold. For some investors, this factor won't be too important. But in the normal course of events, it is preferable to have good liquidity across your portfolio just in case you require funds or wish to make changes to your investments in a timely manner. Investments that are on the share market in companies or listed property trusts and most managed funds are generally liquid. This is a factor that you should consider.

Active and passive investment:

There are two broad forms of investment styles for managed investments such as managed funds: active and passive (or index) investments. Active versus passive investment approaches have been the source of much debate, and both have their advantages and disadvantages. Realise that neither one is right or wrong and both have their place.

So, what is active and passive investment?

Passive management seeks to replicate the market in the asset class it operates through holding investments in the index. For example, for Australian shares, a passive or index manager will hold investments that replicate the ASX200, which you may see on the news as an index that is commonly reported on. This is anticipated to give you a market return and is done for a low cost. It is simple and there is no other science involved.

An active investment manager makes specific investments with an objective of outperforming the market or the index in which it operates. An investment portfolio with this approach will give you the chance but not the guarantee of a better return than the index. One other approach that has some validity is an active manager who seeks a market return for a lower risk (or with lower volatility) than the index. Because active management involves research and investment decision making, these funds are typically more expensive in comparison with passive index funds.

Most research suggests that, of all active fund managers around, **only the top quartile will reach their objective of outperforming the index**. Outperforming the index can be difficult, but not impossible, to do over the long term.

To add some colour to this discussion, to what degree active or passive investment mandates make depends, to some degree, on the asset class or sub-asset class (such as small cap shares) you are talking about. For example, the Australian share market and the ASX200 index is largely dominated by four major banks and two big mining companies. So, you could justifiably argue that, for this asset class, an investment in the index has an element of **concentration** risk in these companies. Therefore, the case for high-quality active management in Australian shares is strong. It is still important to be **brutally** selective with which active fund managers are used.

Other asset classes may involve different decisions for the selection of style. The important point is to consider, based on reasonable assumptions, what is likely to give a sound return net of fees and tax whilst minimising risk.

As mentioned, neither active or passive investment styles are wrong and it can be that you have a mix of both styles.

"So, index investing tracks market indices, is low cost and will give you a market outcome, but most active investing gives you the chance of potentially outperforming the market index without guarantee, right?" Lucy asked to make sure she understood correctly.

"Yes!" said Uncle Alfred, cupping his hands together.

Asset classes and things to know:

1) *Investing in shares:*

Many people have a level of fear about shares. Let's explore what an investment in shares is all about and describe the basic characteristics that we should look for. So, what are shares? Buying shares gives you a part ownership in a business. For example, if you purchase Commonwealth Bank shares, you are a part owner of the business. Similar to if you started your own business, in holding this investment, you are looking for some income from your ownership and for the value of your ownership to rise over time. Therefore, this relates very importantly to how the business performs and what is happening in the business itself. Remember this.

The stock exchange (such as the ASX200) is a marketplace enabling the purchase and sale of part-ownership in businesses that are listed on the exchange. The stock market is, at times, influenced by sentiment which arises from human emotions and the mainstream thinking of the day on what is happening in economies around the world. The more important factor is what is actually happening in the underlying business. At times, the stock market may misprice the actual value of a business per share, which can give rise to opportunity.

Warren Buffett, has used an analogy for explaining the stock market as "Mr. Market", which we share (paraphrased) below.

> The concept of "Mr. Market" is a useful analogy, as used by Ben Graham and Warren Buffett. This helps us to better understand share markets and provides useful guidance towards the aim of profiting from equity markets as opposed to falling victim to "market psychology".
>
> Benjamin Graham, in his book *The Intelligent Investor* (in 1949) used the term "Mr. Market". As a student of Ben Graham, Buffett has referred to this on more than one occasion, including in his annual reports to his investors in the USA. To paraphrase this concept for your benefit, imagine that Mr. Market is a person who provides the ability to buy and sell a company for you.
>
> Unfortunately, Mr. Market has incurable emotional problems.

> At times, he is euphoric and can only see favourable factors affecting the business and, at such times in the state of euphoria, names a very high price for you to buy said company. At other times, Mr. Market is depressed and can see nothing but trouble for that particular business and the world and is wondering, in fact, if the world will end. At such times, he will offer the same business at a very low price because he is gripped with pessimism and fear. Now, the economic fundamentals of this business may be very sound and stable from one day to the next, but Mr. Market's quotations for the price of a share in the business will be anything but.

Ultimately, as Warren Buffett says, Mr. Market has an endearing quality – he doesn't mind being ignored. If his quotation is uninteresting to you today, he will be back with another one tomorrow. **Transactions are strictly at your option**. Beware, Mr. Market is there to serve you, not to guide you. Take advantage of Mr. Market when it is of benefit to you, and ignore him when it is not, all the while keeping an understanding and valuation of what the fundamental intrinsic value of the company in question is.

In reference to this concept, Warren Buffett said, in his annual letter to shareholders in 1987:

> *"...[A]n investor will succeed by coupling good business judgement with an ability to insulate his/her thoughts*

and behaviour from the super contagious emotions that swirl about the marketplace. In my own efforts to stay insulated, I have found it highly useful to keep Ben Graham's Mr. Market concept firmly in mind."

There are some important characteristics to assess in order to understand which businesses are worth investing in when looking at share investments. These are:

- Is the business a strong business, making a profit and are these profits growing?
- Does the business have quality, capable management in place?
- Is it reasonable to expect that the business will be as profitable 10 or 20 years down the track?
- Do they have sound financial characteristics such as reasonable debt levels and a strong balance sheet?
- Do they have a competitive advantage in their business and are they a leading or future leading business in their field?

2) *What key characteristics should you expect from shares?*

- Over a long period of time, shares can provide a strong return.
- An investment in shares should be done with a long-term time horizon, given the fact that markets move up and down and short-term fluctuations are difficult to predict. The medium- to long-term future of the business is easier, although not certain, to estimate.

- Shares tend to be more volatile (price fluctuating up and down) than other types of investments.
- They are highly liquid in most cases.
- Shares will eventually reflect the fundamental value of the underlying business on offer, though not always, and will sometimes be mispriced.
- Shares can be invested in directly through the stock exchange or through a managed fund which holds a portfolio of shares that you buy units in.

"So, shares are basically an ownership in a business that is listed on an exchange, which is a marketplace to buy and sell part ownership in different businesses. When investing, you should understand what is happening in that business to know if it is a good thing to invest in. Or use the managed funds that you talked about before, by buying one that does this for you, selects quality companies and monitors them," Lucy queried, checking that she had understood correctly.

"Spot on, Lucy!" Uncle Alfred exclaimed.

3) *Property and infrastructure:*

Property is an asset class that most people understand better. In a diversified portfolio, the exposure to property is typically via listed real estate trusts (REIT's) or managed funds which provide access to property investments. This provides investors with a share in a pooled portfolio of properties that generate rental income, which is provided to investors. For example, you can have a $10,000 property investment as opposed to holding one specific property which would require a significant amount of capital, such as $400,000, to buy one physical residential investment property. Listed property investments are more liquid, provide a sound income and exposure to capital growth. As a different asset class, it provides diversification. It is important to note that, despite this, some listed real estate trusts experienced significant declines during the global financial crisis, so they are not immune to having negative returns in some periods of time.

Infrastructure is often grouped with property and is a sub-asset class that some would not think of including in their portfolio. Infrastructure includes utilities and facilities that provide essential services. For example, toll roads, airports, utilities such as electricity, and similar. Infrastructure is considered as a growth asset with some defensive attributes. Typically, you would expect:

- Lower volatility compared to other asset classes.
- Infrastructure assets tend to have long-term stable cash flows.
- There are significant barriers to entry and these assets generally have a dominant market position.
- Stable long-term yields with the potential for capital growth.
- Defensive characteristics that come from the provision of essential services.

The vehicle for investing in infrastructure can be directly through the stock exchange or through holding a specialist managed fund which holds a portfolio of listed infrastructure assets. This has a place in a diversified portfolio.

4) *Fixed-interest investments:*

Fixed interest is one of the least understood areas for investments and can get rather complicated. In simple terms, a fixed-interest investment can be a term deposit, which provides a fixed income return and no capital gain or loss, and it can also be through other debt-funded instruments such as government bonds. Fixed-interest investments tend to be defensive and conservative in nature.

If you invest in a government bond for $1,000, you effectively loan $1,000 to the government in return for a series of income payments. At the end of the term, the government gives you the loaned money back. That is what a bond is. In practice, most people have access to a diversified bond portfolio through managed funds, so most people's actual portfolios won't operate with fixed interest quite this simplistically.

The price of a bond before maturing changes with interest rates and moves inversely to interest rate movements. Therefore, bonds perform best in a booming economy with high interest rates when the stock market crashes in a downturn – in a high-interest rate environment that turns into a declining-interest rate environment.

Bonds do offer the potential to earn some element of capital gain (or capital loss), albeit mostly lower than shares would offer. So, this type of fixed interest is fundamentally different to term deposits. History shows, over a long period of time, that bonds should outperform term deposits but, at various points in the economic cycle, this may not be the case. People in Australia generally don't tend to use bonds as much as overseas, perhaps because of unfamiliarity with them. In a diversified portfolio, they have their place in helping reduce the portfolio drawdown concept discussed earlier. Some high-quality, diversified, fixed-interest managed funds can have long-term returns averaging 6% to 7%, which is definitely a positive attribute!

"Right, that's interesting and all new to me, Uncle Alfred. Out of interest, since you said that bonds can potentially provide good returns during a stock market crash, what was it like during the global financial crisis? What types of annual returns were the best bond managed funds providing?" Max asked.

"Great question," Uncle Alfred responded. "I don't have the exact numbers, but I can remember from my portfolio that it was between 8% and 10%."

"That's pretty good, isn't it? For a conservative investment?" Max asked.

"Yes, it is. That's why they have their place. Remember, though, that this was the ideal market environment for bonds," Uncle Alfred cautioned.

5) *Cash:*

Cash is highly liquid, and a cash account provides a level of income and no capital gain. Over the long term, if you had all of your money in cash over many years, it is likely to lose real value as a result of inflation. Inflation is where normal costs associated with everyday life get more expensive. Most of the time, one expects inflation each year.

So, cash really isn't a long-term investment, though you should always have some amount of cash available to you.

Lesson Eight: Things to consider in buying a home

Given Max and Lucy were looking at buying a home, they thought to raise this subject and see what pointers they could get.

Max and Lucy had written a pile of notes and had a zealous, exuberant energy about them through the meaningful addition to their knowledge during the weekend. Max was now feeling optimistic about what his financial future held, something he had not felt for some time.

For many people, buying a home is one of the biggest purchases they will make. Ultimately, purchasing a home is a sound thing to do as long as you have home ownership as an ambition. You should ask yourself if owning a home makes sense for your particular circumstances instead of just forging ahead on the loose idea that everyone does this. Many people will say that renting is "dead money". However, there can be many benefits to renting. So, be clear on whether or not home ownership is a good thing for you specifically.

Here are some things to consider with home ownership:

1) Buy a property that you can afford. Work out your budget and potential monthly repayments of a loan versus what you pay in rent, and ensure that it is affordable to you. Conventional wisdom says that, if you are spending more than 30% of your gross monthly income on mortgage repayments, it is classified as

mortgage stress. In other words, it becomes harder to cover your total cost of living and have money for other things in life, including savings and other investments.

2) Consider if the property market is particularly overheated at the time, and how this might influence your decision to buy. You may decide to wait for a while in this circumstance if feasible. If property markets in your area have risen by more than 15% in recent years, this will tend to be a growth rate that is not sustainable over a medium or long term and the prices may come back. Therefore, consider if it makes sense in these market conditions to buy or wait on the sidelines and keep saving. Conversely, if property prices have been falling and there is the opposite market situation in place, consider how you can take advantage of this.

3) Have a deposit. It is fundamental, but many people often seem to have developed temporary amnesia about this idea. Save some money and ensure that the bank doesn't own all of the property! The ideal deposit is 20% or more. At times, it may not be feasible to get to this level, but the more deposit you have the better.

4) When purchasing a property, negotiate as much as you can. If you are able to get a particular property for 10% less than other surrounding houses, you will already be one step ahead. So, do your best to negotiate.

5) Do your homework on the property or properties you are looking at. Points to think about include:

   a. Have you had a building inspection and pest inspection on the property? It is a good idea to do so.

   b. Know the market in which you are looking. You can access sales and market history through various research providers to assist with this and often a finance broker will have access to one of these providers.

   c. What about the factors that can positively affect the property price moving forward? Does it have good access to public transport? What is the zoning for the property? How good is the location of the property? Are there good schools and amenities in the area? Is it close to or has easy access to the city? Are there planned infrastructure projects that will benefit the area? Are there nice parks, gardens or favourable lifestyle aspects such as a river, beach, or nice commercial strip nearby? What is the suburb like and are there likely improvements on the way in the future? Is the area safe? What about the specific design of the house – is it conducive to a happy home life?

    d. What are the ongoing expenses to be expected with the property such as rates, body corporate or management fees?

6) In your planning, consider the possibility of interest rate rising to at least 2% above the rate at which they currently are. Can you still afford the property you are looking at? Interest rates rise and fall in line with the Reserve Bank of Australia's settings, depending on economic conditions. So, remember that your starting interest rate may not be how it ends up in a few years' time.

7) It is a great idea to aim to pay off your home loan sooner than the full term, which will often be 25 or 30 years. In doing this, you will potentially save many thousands of dollars of interest.

8) Seek help with getting the best deal with a finance broker, get pre-approval for a loan prior to negotiating any offer to purchase a property and, where required in other areas, seek quality advice to assist you in the process.

Chapter Four
Summary Learning Points:

- Think long term when investing and be patient. In general, there are two things that an investment can provide to varying degrees: income and the value of the investment growing over time, otherwise known as capital growth.
- The power of compound returns is evident the longer the time period of your investment.
- Managed funds are pooled investment vehicles that enable investors to have diversified investments that are managed by professionals.
- Factors relevant in constructing an investment portfolio:
  - Liquidity – how readily the assets can be converted into cash.
  - Diversification – getting a spread of investments.
  - Considering and minimising drawdown risks where possible.
  - Asset allocation – considering what proportions you will have invested in different types of assets.
  - Understanding how much risk you are comfortable in taking with investments and having a portfolio that is consistent with this.

- Index investment is a style which mimics an investment index and basically gives exposure to a market return. Active investing aims to outperform the index in which the investments reside, without guarantee that this will be delivered.
- Shares can provide strong returns over time, though tend to exhibit more volatility in comparison with other types of investments. Shares are an ownership in the underlying business.
- Property investments offer investors with a rental yield a chance for some capital growth and tend to be less volatile in comparison with shares. Infrastructure assets are somewhat monopolistic in nature, tend to have stable and predictable cash flows and include such things as toll roads, airports and utilities.
- Fixed interest investments include things such as term deposits, government or corporate bonds and similar. These should not be overlooked in a diversified portfolio. The price of a bond is inversely related to interest rates and they can potentially make a capital gain (or loss) over time.
- Cash is essential for all, although, over the long term, it is possible for the real value of an investment in cash to be

less than it started with after the effects of inflation are taken into account. Having some cash is necessary as a contingency and to take advantage of opportunities. Cash offers some income with no chance of capital growth and potential for the value being eroded by inflation.

- Home ownership, or buying a property, is a good thing to aspire to, if it is your desire to own a home. Be careful to do your research and consider the eight-step list shown in this chapter prior to buying a home.

Chapter Five

Retirement and superannuation

LESSON NINE: Retirement planning system – Superannuation

In talking about building wealth in general, something to know a little more about is superannuation – the Australian retirement system.

Superannuation is the Australian government's system to assist people in accumulating sufficient resources for retirement. Fundamentally, it is a good system. Similar retirement systems exist overseas to assist people in accumulating funds for retirement, such as the 401k system in the USA. Remember earlier we talked about tax and investing tax effectively being an important contributor to efficiently building wealth? Superannuation is one of the most tax-effective vehicles for investments that exists. Many have a level of scepticism about superannuation and this is largely due to not knowing enough about the system. There is certainly potential for the government to modify the rules. However, the system is a very tax-effective investment vehicle and is highly likely to remain so.

These days, many of the managed investments that you can find outside of super, you can also invest in within super, depending on the super fund and breadth of investment choice. The Australian system and choice of investments out there is well-developed. Of course, care and analysis is always required with any investment.

The main point of superannuation is to enable people to have funds for retirement. So, for this reason, it is deliberately not easily accessible before you get close to the end of your working career, except for in some very particular circumstances. Furthermore, the government, in mandating employers to put money in your super for you, is ensuring that at least some money is going towards your future retirement. In fairness, if this wasn't in place, many people wouldn't be accumulating anything.

"Come to think of it, Uncle Alfred, if I consider my super balance and our current situation, since I haven't yet bought a home, it's the biggest asset I have. And, truthfully, I wouldn't have done this on my own steam, so I guess it's a good thing that I have some funds already there," Max realised.

"You're right, Max. Be clear, though, that the current employer contribution rate of 9.5%, which is most likely what your employer is paying (unless they have a policy of paying a higher rate) **is highly likely not going to be sufficient to**

retire on, even if this has been paid into your fund since you were 22 years old. A higher percentage is required," Uncle Alfred warned.

Some employers provide a higher rate, which is a good benefit. As a general rule of thumb, if you were to start your career and have a 15% to 20% contribution into your super and this continues for your entire working career, it would certainly be a lot closer to providing sufficient resources. Care should be taken to look at your specific situation as this is merely a broad statement.

Take an interest in your super, it **is** your money and it is highly likely to be one of your biggest assets. Understand how much you have, how it is invested, and if you realise that you want some advice to make it work more efficiently towards building a bigger pot for your old age, then go out and seek this from a trusted source.

There are various styles of super funds that all have their place. The main styles include industry super funds, retail super funds, employer funds, and self-managed super funds. They vary from low cost and simple investment options to having a wide variety of investment options as well as insurance options within super. Superannuation has become a very competitive industry and there are high-quality funds that exist in these styles. Nowadays, almost everyone can choose which super fund they wish to have. You should consider which aspects of a super fund matter to you, such as wanting a wide array of investment options at a reasonable cost.

There are two types of contributions that you can make into super, and two different limits related to how much you can deposit. They are known as concessional (before tax) contributions and non-concessional (after tax) contributions. The limits on these tend to be updated **every couple of years**, so it's a good idea to check the limit for the current year to ensure that you are up to date.

Concessional super contributions:

Concessional super contributions are any contributions made by your employer or from your salary **before** your PAYG tax is deducted.

They include the following:

- Employer Superannuation Guarantee (SG) contributions.
- Salary sacrifice contributions.
- Employer-paid insurance premiums.
- Personal contributions for which you have claimed a tax deduction.

These include the contributions paid by your employer at 9.5% or higher.

These concessional (or pre-tax) contributions within the contribution limit are taxed at 15% in most cases, unless you earn over the high-income limit, currently $300,000, and this will be dropped to $250,000 from 1 July 2017, in which case the tax is 30%. For many people, unless you are on a low income, this means that concessional contributions can be tax-effective. There are two components of your super account: taxable and tax free. Concessional contributions like those mentioned above fall into the taxable component classification.

A popular strategy to boost your retirement savings is known as salary sacrifice to super. In the right circumstances, for the right people, this can be an effective strategy. If you "sacrifice" some of your income to your super via salary sacrifice, it means that instead of receiving your full pay in cash, some of your pay packet is directed to make additional (concessional) contributions to super. Depending on your marginal tax rate, this can be a way to get more benefit out of your income.

Non-concessional super contributions:

These are any contributions made from your after-tax salary.

Non-concessional contributions within the contribution limit are not taxed by your super fund because it is already coming from after-tax money and they are included in your tax-free component within your super account.

By making post-tax contributions to your super, you might be eligible for what is known as the government co-contribution scheme.

"We will talk more about different types of contributions into the superannuation system after dinner, but for now, let's move on," Uncle Alfred explained.

Lesson Ten: How much is enough for retirement?

"How much will I need for my retirement? I've got no idea of what amount I should be aiming for." This is an age-old question for which there is no single answer!

It depends on your circumstances and the income that you wish to draw each year in retirement. Refer to the concepts of financial security and financial freedom in Lesson Three. An example was given for one couple, indicating their costs for the **basics** of living and for their all-inclusive cost of living. At retirement, they should have paid off their mortgage, so this amount could potentially be removed from their lifestyle expenditure. Be aware that these figures will be different depending on your requirements. If you can work out the income that you wish to draw in retirement, then I can give you a simple rule of thumb to estimate the nest egg required. This is as a guide **only** and assumes there is no part-pension from Australia's social security system, Centrelink. If you receive this part-pension, then you potentially don't require as much for your nest egg. To be conservative, it's best to assume that this isn't the case.

Because many are unsure about how much income they would require, assuming that their home is paid off, the Association of Super Funds Australia (ASFA), published some statistics on what comfortable lifestyle requirements are on average in Australia.[5] Make sure that you only use these as a guide. Ideally, you will have as much income as possible in retirement. This suggests that a couple with a comfortable lifestyle will require an income of $59,000 per annum. As a rule of thumb, for a sustainable balance in retirement, you can multiply this figure by 20 (or divide by 5%) to get a required lump sum, which works out to be $1,180,000 or roughly $1.2 million in today's dollar terms.

If you want to pass on your nest egg to the next generation, then you will be looking to draw just an income from it, rather than depleting the capital value too much. Various pieces of research suggest that a sustainable percentage of income can be 3% to 5% to maintain the nest egg value. The above rule assumes a 5% income, but be aware of the trend that people are living longer and that it is possible that, at a 5% income amount, the nest egg slowly reduces in value over the course of retirement and can possibly deplete fully, depending on investment returns and longevity.

"Okay, thanks, Uncle Alfred. So, there is a rule of thumb that can help with a lump-sum amount that Max and I would need and, from what you said before, this is a financial freedom goal as opposed to covering the basics or a financial security amount. So, for example, if I said our basic living costs

---

[5] **Source:** https://www.superannuation.asn.au/resources/retirement-standard

are $30,000 for basic bills, food and accommodation, then that first hurdle is $600,000 for financial security, right? And what you just said is for not having to work at all, right?" Lucy asked.

"Yes, good point Lucy, that's right," Uncle Alfred agreed.

Chapter Five
Summary Learning Points:

- Superannuation is the Australian retirement system and is a vehicle for investing that is very tax effective.
- The purpose of superannuation is to accumulate and eventually provide income for retirement.
- There are two types of contributions that can be made, with different limit rules for each: concessional (before tax) contributions and non-concessional (after tax) contributions.
- Some types of superannuation contributions that can be of value include:
    - Salary sacrifice.
    - Spouse super contributions.
    - Government co-contribution.
- In attempting to estimate how much you will require in retirement, first understand the income per year that you would like or will need. Then, as a rule of thumb, multiply the amount by 20. This will give you a rough idea of the lump sum required to generate this income. This is a simple way to get to a figure, but be aware that this may not be exact.

Chapter Six

Family-related planning

LESSON ELEVEN: Giving your kids a head-start with money

After Max, Lucy, Uncle Alfred, Jo and Darcy spent a nice couple of hours on an extended walk, they all returned to the house and had some afternoon tea before another session of learning was to take place.

"Max, you mentioned earlier that Lucy and you are looking to have kids at some point. We talked before and provided an example that shows how compound returns can really work in your favour over time, which is a great lesson to pass on. Let me add to that topic of teaching your kids about money," Uncle Alfred said.

Teaching your kids good money habits:

As a parent, you are a role model for your kids. So, use the principles and ideas in what we have talked about, Max, and make positive changes for yourself as this will rub off on your kids in the future. They are impressionable and will be absorbing what you do, whether you realise it or not. Furthermore, as a lot of schools don't teach good money habits, passing on this education to them as a parent is potentially a very valuable life skill. Think about how you can do this effectively with your kids. This could be one of the most important things that you will pass on to them so that they can look after themselves in the future.

One way you can help them in getting used to the concept of saving and delayed gratification is this: when your child receives birthday money or money from a grandparent, aunt or otherwise, keep 50% of the money for them and deposit it in a savings account. Then, you could potentially invest this money for them over time, which is a great idea. The other 50% is provided to your child for something that they may want. Done consistently over time, this will embed the idea of saving and investing early on and will also help in building wealth from a very early age. Remember, the earlier you start the better, so it is a great idea.

An alternative model that is a little more involved is presented here for you to think about as well. In the same scenario when money is given to your child or you provide pocket money to them, then you can allocate it like this:

- ◆ 25% of the funds is provided to charity that they help in choosing.

- 25% of the funds is given to them as "something for now".
- 25% of the funds is provided to your child as savings for something specific that they want in the future.
- 25% of the funds is invested for your child.

Depending on the amount given to them, the breakdown may be small amounts, however it is still a powerful way to teach them the fundamentals.

These are only two models that can work – there are others. But the point is to make sure that you think about how you teach your kids about money and, more importantly, set a good example for them to follow. This can be an extra incentive for you to be effective with your money.

Lucy was particularly keen to hear this and ensure that their kids in the future can learn great lessons from home regarding money that will set them on the right path.

Lesson Twelve: Protecting your family

Uncle Alfred turned his attention from the previous lesson to something that tends to be poorly understood or appreciated: protecting your family.

Some say that protection is the foundation of building wealth.

For most people, the word "insurance" conjures negative feelings. Many believe that insurers don't pay in their time of need, but this is the difference between quality insurance and inferior cover. The reality is that family protection, such as life insurance and income protection, is paid out in very large sums every year with quality insurers. So, that's something that you should remember, particularly when you have young children and debts such as a mortgage.

The following points briefly summarise what insurances exist that are relevant to family and asset protection:

Life insurance/death benefit cover:

This refers to the type of insurance where a lump sum is payable to the policy holder in the event of death or terminal illness of the insured person. It is meant to provide for the family that is left behind and to potentially pay out mortgages or liabilities. The amount that is most suitable for you to hold may be a lot more than you think. It is also cheaper than many realise.

Total and permanent disability insurance:

Often called TPD insurance, total and permanent disability insurance refers to a lump sum payment that is provided where a person becomes totally and permanently disabled and is unlikely to ever work again. This is the second kind of personal protection that exists. Some policies provide a payment if you can't work in any occupation and others provide a payment if you can't work in your **specific** usual occupation due to the disability. TPD insurance is intended to help meet the costs of medical treatment, rehabilitation, debt repayments, the future cost of living incurred and assist with the reality that the person, in this instance, will never be going back to work. So, again, it is for a very severe outcome. *Note: the definitions of TPD vary between insurance providers and policy types.*

Income protection insurance:

This provides a monthly income replacement (which is less than 100% of your current income) where you cannot work due to illness or injury (that is you can't work due to health reasons; therefore, it replaces your income). Generally, this benefit is paid via an income stream to you over the period where you are unable to work due to health reasons. Once you can return to work, then the income protection payments cease. There is normally a waiting period and a benefit payment period associated with this cover.

Income protection can involve variations, including a policy which assesses and signs off your income at the application stage (agreed value) or a policy which assesses your income at the claim time and provides you with the sum insured or 75% of your last 12 to 24 months' income (depending on the insurer). An indemnity policy has some risks attached to it and, as such, tends to be cheaper.

As you can see, there are various aspects to consider. Protecting your ability to earn an income is very important in the overall scheme of things, so do not underestimate its importance. If you don't have an income, you can't pay for your home costs, food, car insurance, house insurance and other costs, unless you have substantial assets behind you that provide enough income for this.

Trauma/critical illness insurance:

Trauma and critical illness insurance provides a lump sum payment if a person is diagnosed with a specific trauma condition or is required to undergo a medical procedure that is listed on the policy. These are severe medical trauma events where you will need some financial help to recover from them such as cancer, heart attack, stroke and heart disease. This provides a safety net to cover medical expenses, rehabilitation and debts while you recover.

Those are the four key personal insurances, with a few additional types to consider if you run a business of your own.

Lucy was particularly interested here in ensuring that her and Max were well protected.

These are some basics about protection for your family, but be aware that there is more to it. There tends to be insurances that you are given (**group cover**) as part of a larger group through some super funds that don't involve an underwriting process, and insurances that you apply for that specifically assess you (**personal cover**) and the insurer decides whether to cover you or not. Generally speaking, personal cover tends to have stronger definitions and protection.

Hearing this information, it dawned on Max and Lucy that it was an area they really hadn't considered at all and certainly would in the future.

"I have only one more lesson for you, Lucy and Max, before we summarise and relax for afternoon tea!" Uncle Alfred exclaimed.

Max and Lucy looked at each other with a look of resolve and energy, having benefited greatly from what they had heard.

Lesson Thirteen: Estate planning

Estate planning is getting the right assets to the right people at the right time.

Make no mistake about it: it is one of the things required in getting your financial house in order. Many people have not addressed their needs here, so do yourself a favour and be one of those who has this sorted out!

This could potentially mean providing some funds to intended recipients during your lifetime, so that you get to see them enjoy the benefit, or it can mean owning your home in joint names so that it automatically passes to your partner if you are not around. This is an area where you should really consider your situation and needs, work out what your intentions are in passing assets on to others, then go about addressing the best manner to implement these.

Consider your family situation and if there are any people who are more financially dependent or struggle with money; this may affect how you provide a benefit to them or any other family-related issues to handle. With estate planning, you should consider your entire situation. Having a Will and an enduring power of attorney in place is a starting point, but by no means covers your whole situation.

You should understand that, sometimes, not all assets flow through your Will and can bypass it completely.

In families, there are often some who aren't good with money who you would like to provide for. Carefully think about the best manner in which to do this. For example, if you have a son or daughter in the future that falls into this category, you may wish to provide them with some funds, but mandate that it is used as a deposit on their first home so that the money doesn't just pass through their hands.

An alternative option where there are sufficient assets to justify is to look at a particular trust, which is capital protected, or has the right Trustees in place if it isn't so that they can be managed for the Beneficiaries' best interests. A capital-protected trust is set up so that the Beneficiary(s) can have the good fortune of the income from the trust, but cannot touch any of the capital or assets within it. Every family is slightly different, so it is important to think about your situation and discuss it with your partner and an estate-planning lawyer to cover the right scenarios and options for you.

Here is a checklist of things that you should consider with estate planning:

1) Consider the ownership names of your assets – either joint names, individual, family trust, alternative type of trust, company names or otherwise. Think about what happens to the assets if you are not around and what you wish to happen with them. Family Trusts, for example, will endure beyond death and can be an ongoing vehicle to manage financial resources. Who will be the Trustees if you are unable to perform this role? It pays to seek specialist advice where necessary on the relevance of different structures in your situation.

2) Consider the intended Beneficiaries. How do you wish to pass on benefits to them? During your lifetime? When they hit a certain age? When you are no longer around? Do you need to safeguard their interests and think about how you provide a benefit to them?

3) Have a Will and enduring power of attorney in place to reflect your intentions. This is best done with a qualified solicitor who can direct you on the best manner to draft your documents. There are other ways to have your Will done, including the Public Trustee's office in your state. If you have managed to accumulate significant resources, ask your lawyer about whether a testamentary trust is relevant for your situation.

4) Keep estate planning documents in a safe place and let key people in the family know about them.

5) Have discussions within the family unit so that your intentions are understood and to avoid the chance of future challenges to your estate.

6) Make sure that you have correctly done your superannuation nominations and, unless there is a good reason to the contrary, consider binding nominations for estate planning certainty.

7) If you own a business, consider the estate planning implications of this and have a plan for this in place.

"Wow, there are some really important topics in there that I didn't even consider at all! So, just to check, a Will is a legal document to record what you want to happen with your estate when you are no longer alive, right? So, what is an enduring power of attorney? Is that where I nominate someone who is highly trusted by me who can handle my financial affairs if I am unable to?" Lucy queried.

"Good questions Lucy. Yes, you are right," Uncle Alfred replied. "The enduring power of attorney is a legal document where you nominate a trusted person to make financial and property decisions for you. This can be active either in the instance of incapacity or if the person is in a coma, for example, or even if they just happen to be overseas. You can also have more than one power of attorney. A Will is a legal document that clearly sets out your wishes for the distribution of your assets after your death. It is important that both documents are valid and up to date."

Lucy had written down some notes on this subject and learnt something here that estate planning is about a lot more than just a Will. Max realised that this was something he needed to discuss with Lucy and decided to sketch a family tree on one piece of paper to trigger a full family context of the discussion.

Chapter Six
Summary Learning Points:

- Consider how you will teach your kids good money habits from a very young age. Two models of teaching children about money have been provided in this chapter, which both involve children understanding that not all money is to be spent right here and now.
- Protecting the family and yourself through high-quality insurance is important. Four key insurances exist for this:
  - Life insurance – provides a lump sum on death or terminal illness.
  - Total and permanent disability – provides a lump sum to cover not being able to ever return to work again.
  - Income protection – protects your ability to earn an income where you are unable to due to health reasons.
  - Trauma or critical illness cover – provides a lump sum to help with severe medical traumas that are expensive to recuperate from.
- Estate planning is about having the right assets pass to the right hands at the right time and should not be forgotten in getting your financial "house in order".

- With your estate planning, you should consider your particular situation and needs, what your intentions are, and seek specialist advice on the best way to implement those.
- Refer to the checklist provided for things to consider with your estate planning.

Putting it all together

At this point, Uncle Alfred paused and realised that this was the last of what he wished to get across to Max and Lucy. A beaming smile spread across his face with a noticeable warmth and caring energy emanating from within.

"Well, Lucy and Max, those are all the lessons I have for you. Since we started, I have noticed a noticeable shift in your body language and demeanour to a positive state and that is fantastic. I hope that this has been helpful," Uncle Alfred said.

"Absolutely, that was incredibly helpful and Max and I cannot thank you enough. This knowledge is truly a gift that you have given us. Thank you!" Lucy shared with overwhelming gratitude.

So, Max, Lucy, Uncle Alfred, and their hosts turned their attention to enjoying the rest of their weekend. Max and Lucy were really inspired and decided to start by seizing the moment and changing things for the better the day they returned. They were excited for the future and Max's feelings of stress were greatly reduced and he could now see a way forward.

To summarise, Max and Lucy learnt about the following on their weekend away:

- Money psychology and how important this is. Their mindsets were challenged and they were really inspired to act and make a positive change.
- Money rules to live by and the concept of positive rituals to build progress and effective goal-setting.
- Building wealth and what you can do to accelerate this, making good financial decisions, and exploring investing in more depth, including different types of assets that you can invest in and their characteristics.
- Superannuation as the main way to invest for retirement and how to estimate how much you need to retire.
- Teaching children good money habits, financial protection through insurance and estate planning.

These lessons considerably opened their eyes to things that they hadn't thought of previously.

Max was feeling positively inspired – a marked difference to his mood on arrival to visit his friends. When he chatted to Lucy later with all the exuberance of a school boy, she was really happy to hear the excitement in his voice and, in that moment, felt close to her husband, given the fervour and love that she had for him and how he was directing towards giving them a better future. This was a weekend that they would never forget because of the unexpected lessons they learnt from the kindness and wisdom of Uncle Alfred.

Max was a changed man and Lucy was armed with knowledge – their future would be forever brighter for the positive actions they were about to take.

May it also be so for you.

Bonus Chapter

If you feel inspired and eager to learn more, this bonus chapter has additional information for your benefit. It goes into further depth in some areas, as part of the deeper conversations Uncle Alfred had with Max and Lucy.

Below is a life expenditure plan template, which you can use for identifying what expenditure plan you choose to set in your own personal life. Once you have finalised a plan, you should track your progress so that you know how you are going in working towards this. This is a key element that many don't get around to doing. I challenge you to be different!

FIDO'S Lifestyle expenditure planner

1. Choose a weekly, fortnightly, monthly or yearly plan.
2. Convert all amounts to match your plan. Use our converter.
3. Type in the cells with black figures only. Cells with coloured figures are subtotals and totals and are calculated for you; leave these untouched.
4. Totals shown in blue are income amounts; totals shown in red are expense amounts.

CONVERTER	from	to
annual amount:	$0	
quarterly amount	$0	
per week	$0	
per fortnight	$0	
per month	$0	

START HERE

Section A: Income after tax

Your after tax income	$0
Partner/ spouse after tax income	$0
Pension/ benefit	$0
Family payment	$0
Child support received	$0
Board money received	$0
Investments (after tax)	$0
Other income (after tax)	$0
TOTAL INCOME	$0

Section B: Expenses
Housing

	Rent	$0
	1st mortgage	$0
	2nd mortgage	$0
	Land rates	$0
	Water rates	$0
	House and contents insurance	$0
	House repairs	$0
	Strata levies	$0
	Home contents replacements	$0

Utilities

	Electricity	$0
	Heating oil	$0
	Gas	$0
	Water	$0
	Mobile phone	$0
	Internet and Cable TV	$0
	Telephone	$0

Transport

	Petrol	$0
	Repairs	$0
	Registration	$0
	Fines	$0
	Insurance	$0
	Licence	$0
	Fares	$0

Food

	Groceries	$0
	Meat	$0
	Fruit/Vegetables	$0
	Lunches	$0
	Pet Food	$0
	Take away food/ restaurants	$0

Education

School Fees	$0
Uniforms	$0
Self Education	$0
School excursions	$0
Tutoring/Books	$0
Sports/out of school activities	$0
Pre-school	$0
Child minding	$0

Medical

Health insurance	$0
Doctor	$0
Dentist	$0
Chemist	$0
Eye care and optometrist	$0
Specialists/alternative therapies	$0
Pet and vet	$0

Maintenance

Children	$0

Personal

Clothing	$0
Haircuts	$0
Grooming/cosmetics	$0
Entertainment	$0
Sport	$0
Club fees	$0
Newspaper and Magazines	$0
Holidays	$0
Gifts	$0
Pocket money – children	$0
Drinks alcoholic	$0
Cigarettes/Tobacco	$0

Laundry/dry cleaning	$0
Gambling/other	$0
Donations/other	$0
DVDs/Videos/Movies	$0
Postage/Films	$0
Pool/Gardening Expenses	$0

Other

Superannuation	$0
Life/term/income Insurance	$0
Professional fees	$0
Other expenditure	$0
Savings	$0
Special Projects	$0
Total basic living expenses	$0

Section C: Your loan expenses

Credit Cards	$0
	$0
	$0
	$0
Personal loans	$0
	$0
	$0
Car Loans/Hire purchase	$0
	$0
Store cards/accounts	$0
	$0
	$0
Home loans	$0
Other debts	$0

Total loan expenses $0

TOTAL ALL EXPENDITURE $0

HOW MUCH TO REPAY A LOAN?	
Amount to repay	$
Annual interest rate	0.00%
Choose weeks to repay	0
Amount to pay off per week	$0
Convert weeks to:	0
months	0
year	0

Your bottom line

Your after tax income (from section A) $0

Less your living expenses (from section B) $0

Less your loan expenses (from section C) $0

Equals either a surplus (in blue) or deficit (in red) $0

Now you know that you're spending your money on, you can plan to get your expenses under control.

Read our tips on keeeping to your plan so you can find extra money to spend.
www.fido.asic.gov.au

ASIC
Australian Securities & Investments Commission

Risks to retirement income

Many sources suggest that we should anticipate that we will have longer life expectancies in the future. In retirement years, the longer one lives, the more real the possibility that one outlives their money becomes. This is otherwise known as a longevity risk.

There are several variables that come into play, including the returns generated by your retirement fund and the amount that you withdraw as income payments on an ongoing basis. In terms of the probability of outliving your money, it is a very real possibility for some.

The table below that's related to longevity risk indicates the portfolio success rates based on the percentage withdrawal rate and time in income drawdown phase. You may notice how the longer one lives, the less positive the portfolio success rates are.

Portfolio success rates

Withdrawal rate as a percentage of initial portfolio value

Payout	1%	2%	3%	4%	5%	6%	7%	8%	9%	10%
100% stocks										
10 yrs	100%	100%	100%	100%	100%	99%	96%	96%	95%	90%
20 yrs	100%	100%	100%	98%	96%	91%	76%	64%	51%	33%
30 yrs	100%	100%	100%	96%	90%	72%	61%	45%	27%	16%
40 yrs	100%	100%	100%	94%	79%	63%	50%	32%	21%	11%
75% stocks/20% bonds/5% bills										
10 yrs	100%	100%	100%	100%	100%	99%	98%	95%	93%	87%
20 yrs	100%	100%	100%	98%	93%	85%	65%	52%	41%	24%
30 yrs	100%	100%	99%	95%	77%	61%	41%	27%	17%	9%
40 yrs	100%	100%	97%	88%	60%	50%	26%	18%	8%	4%
50% stocks/45% bonds/5% bills										
10 yrs	100%	100%	100%	100%	100%	100%	98%	93%	86%	82%
20 yrs	100%	100%	100%	98%	88%	67%	53%	40%	29%	21%
30 yrs	100%	100%	99%	82%	60%	37%	27%	17%	7%	5%
40 yrs	100%	100%	93%	58%	40%	28%	17%	7%	41%	1%
25% stocks/70% bonds/5% bills										
10 yrs	100%	100%	100%	100%	100%	100%	97%	89%	82%	76%
20 yrs	100%	100%	100%	88%	67%	51%	36%	30%	27%	18%
30 yrs	100%	100%	85%	56%	33%	28%	17%	10%	6%	2%
40 yrs	100%	94%	63%	33%	24%	11%	6%	3%	1%	0%

Portfolio success rates									
Withdrawal rate as a percentage of initial portfolio value									
Payout	1%	2%	3%	4%	5%	6%	7%	8%	9%	10%
95% bonds/5% bills									
10 yrs	100%	100%	100%	100%	100%	95%	92%	81%	71%	58%
20 yrs	100%	100%	93%	67%	48%	35%	29%	28%	26%	16%
30 yrs	100%	90%	49%	33%	26%	18%	10%	6%	2%	2%
40 yrs	100%	72%	32%	24%	8%	4%	1%	1%	0%	0%

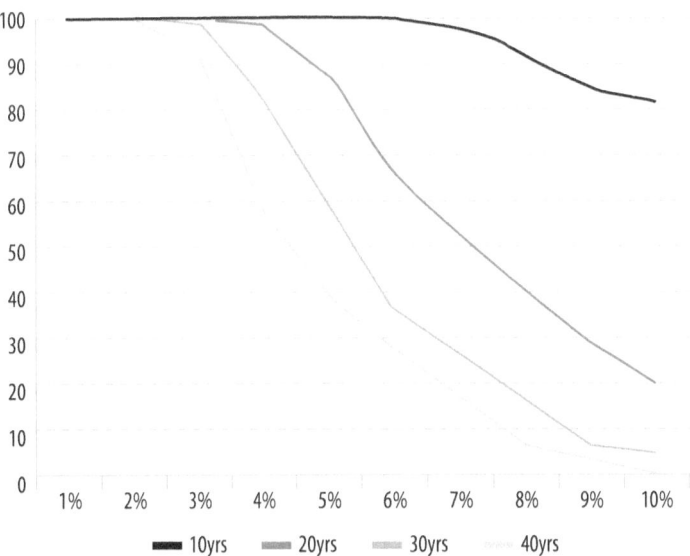

Portfolio success rates comparison

(Source for above graphs: Drew, M, and Walk, A, (2014), How Safe are Safe Withdrawal Rates in Retirement? An Australian Perspective, Finsia (Financial Services Institute of Australasia), Sydney.)

In retirement, the sequencing risk or the pattern in which returns are generated, particularly immediately upon retirement, can also influence how long your retirement fund lasts. No discussion and education about retirement is complete without highlighting this point.

Example of the possible impact of sequencing risk in retirement using Australian market performance data

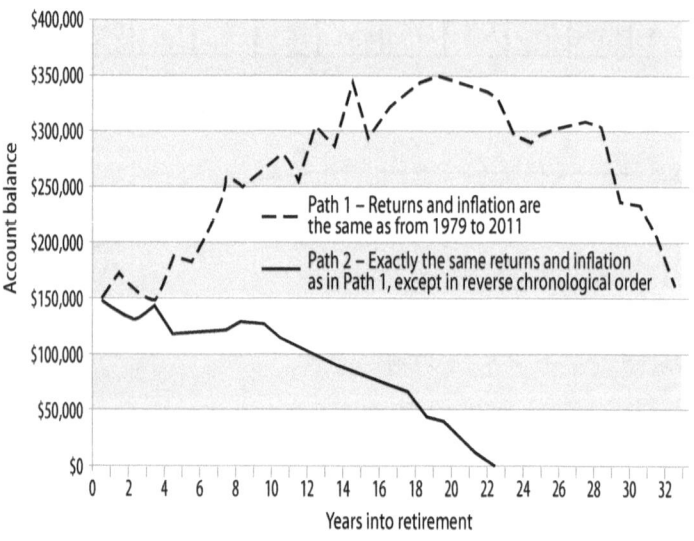

Source: Challenger Life Company Limited estimates based on data from Bloomberg.

SEQUENCE OF RETURNS
Impact During Savings

BLACKROCK®

The sequence of returns has no impact on the final portfolio value when you are saving.
- Three investors made the same initial hypothetical investment of $1,000,000 at age 40 with no additions or withdrawals.
- All had an average annual return of 7% over 25 years. However, each experienced a different sequence of returns.
- At age 65, all had the same portfolio value, although they had experienced different valuations along the way.

THREE UNIQUE RETURN SCENARIOS

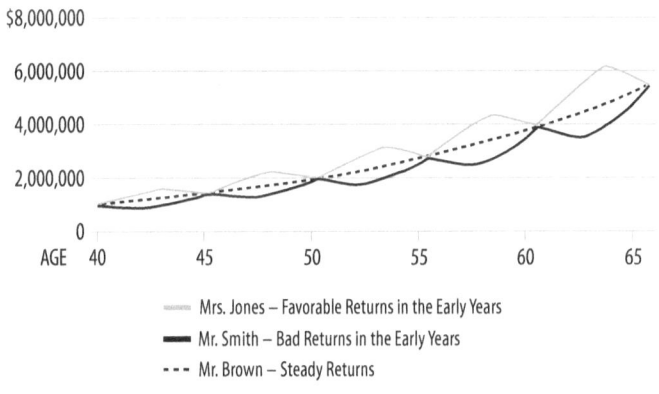

- Mrs. Jones – Favorable Returns in the Early Years
- **Mr. Smith – Bad Returns in the Early Years**
- - - Mr. Brown – Steady Returns

Source: BlackRock. This graphic looks at the effect the sequence of returns can have on your portfolio value over a long period of time. Other factors that may affect the longevity of assets include the investment mix, taxes and expenses related to investing. This is a hypothetical illustration. This illustration assumes a hypothetical initial portfolio balance of $1,000,000 with no additions or withdrawals and the hypothetical sequence of returns noted in the table. These figures are for illustrative purposes only and do not represent any particular investment, nor do they reflect any investment fees, expenses or taxes.

SEQUENCE OF RETURNS
Impact during withdrawal

The sequence of returns can have a critical impact on portfolio value when you are withdrawing due to the compounding effect on the annual account balances and annual withdrawals.

- Three investors made the same initial hypothetical investment of $1,000,000 upon retirement at age 65.
- All had an average annual return of 7% over 25 years, which followed the same sequences as during the savings phase.
- All made withdrawals of $60,000, adjusted annually for inflation.
- At age 90, all had different portfolio values due to annual withdrawal.

THREE UNIQUE RETURN SCENARIOS

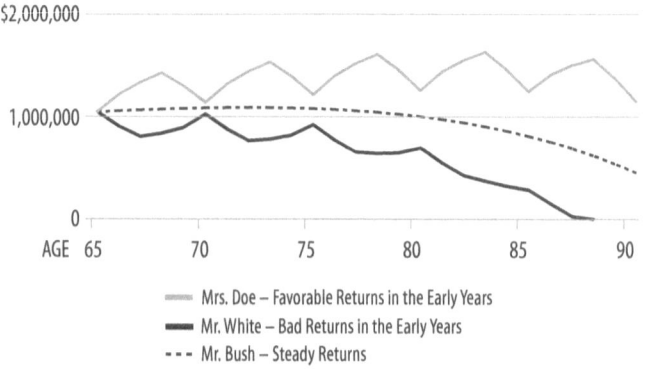

— Mrs. Doe – Favorable Returns in the Early Years
— Mr. White – Bad Returns in the Early Years
--- Mr. Bush – Steady Returns

Source: BlackRock. This graphic looks at the effect the sequence of returns can have on your portfolio value over a long period of time. Other factors that may affect the longevity of assets include the investment mix, taxes, expenses related to investing and the number of years of retirement funding (life expectancy). This is a hypothetical illustration. This illustration assumes a hypothetical initial portfolio balance of $1,000,000, annual withdrawals of $60,000 adjusted annually by 3% for inflation and the hypothetical sequence of returns noted in the table. These figures are for illustrative purposes only and do not represent any particular investment, nor do they reflect any investment fees, expenses or taxes. When you are withdrawing money from a portfolio, your results can be affected by the sequence of returns even when average return remains the same, due to the compounding effect on the annual account balances and annual withdrawals.

The good news is that there are some solutions to mitigate these risks in retirement. This bonus chapter is not intended to provide all of these solutions, but will focus on annuities. The reason for focussing on one solution is that it is not an option that many know of, but it's one that you should be aware of.

Annuities

When you purchase an annuity, instead of a lump sum of money, you gain the benefit of a guaranteed income either for your lifetime or for a set number of years. This ensures that you will have some income for the rest of your life or for a defined number of years regardless of what happens with your other investments. This is a very conservative style of investment that protects against longevity risk and can provide some assurance of a defined outcome in an uncertain world. Annuities have a place, but may not be appropriate for everyone.

In practice, some will use annuities as a component of a retirement plan to have a "layer" of guaranteed income.

You can buy an annuity from some retirement funds or life insurance companies using your retirement fund money or other savings.

Example:

> Fred is 65 years old and married. He decides to purchase a lifetime annuity and invests $200,000. This annuity will pay him a regular income of $700 per month, increasing with inflation each year, for the rest of his life. He also likes that this annuity has a 10-year guarantee period, ensuring that his wife will receive his income for at least a defined period should he die within those 10 years.

Benefits of annuities:

- Regardless of how markets perform, you are paid a guaranteed income, providing certainty and assurance of a regular income.

- Annuities purchased with superannuation money from age 60 are tax free.

- Annuities purchased with superannuation money before age 60 will have the taxable portion taxed at your marginal tax rate. However, you will receive a 15% offset.

- Only the income component (if any) of an annuity purchased with non-super money is taxable.

- You don't pay tax on investment earnings.

Disadvantages of annuities:

- Money can't be taken out as a lump sum.
- You have no choice in how the annuity funds are invested.
- You may not be able to transfer to an account-based pension.
- Over the long term, an annuity may pay less than a market-linked investment.

Annuity providers tend to give a choice on how often regular payments are received and it is possible to opt for a "reversionary" income recipient so that payments continue to be paid to a Beneficiary when you die. If you are considering annuities, be careful to closely consider if they are right for you.

Therefore, annuities can be a potential solution for longevity risk, alongside other possibilities not covered in this book.

Trusts

What is a Trust?

You may have heard some people talk about having a Trust structure or a Family Trust before. So, what exactly is a Trust? This section is intended to give you a basic understanding of what a Trust is.

A Trust is a relationship where a person (the Trustee) is under an obligation to hold property for the benefit of others (the Beneficiaries). The terms of the obligation are defined by the terms of the Trust Deed that's entered into between the Trustee and the Settlor.

The Trustee is the legal owner of the trust property and the Beneficiaries hold the beneficial interest in the Trust property.

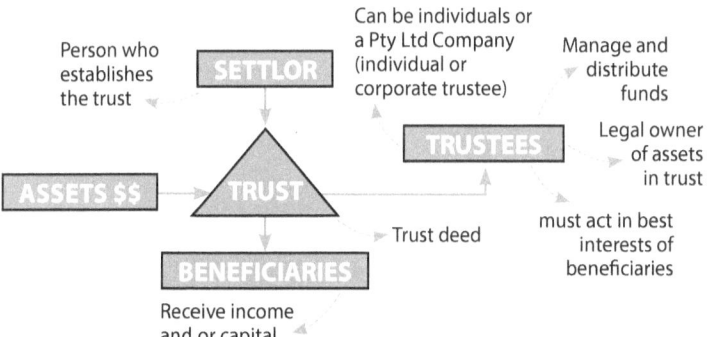

Setting up a Trust

A Trust is usually set up through speaking with an accountant or lawyer. Since there are some complexities existing with a trust, it is a good idea to seek credible advice in this area.

The Trust Deed

The Trust Deed defines the relationship between the Trustee and the Beneficiaries. The key parties to the Trust Deed are the Settlor and the Trustee. The Trust Deed specifically sets out the duties and powers of investment of the Trustee, the Beneficiaries, and other important things.

Discretionary Trusts

In a Discretionary Trust (often called a family trust), the Beneficiaries do not have fixed entitlements or interest in the trust assets. The Trustee has the discretion to determine which of the Beneficiaries are to receive the capital and income of the trust and how much they will receive. The Trustee does not have complete discretion, meaning they can only distribute to Beneficiaries within a nominated class according to the terms of the Trust Deed.

Key parties of a Discretionary Trust:

There are four roles that need to be considered when establishing a Discretionary Trust:

1) *The Settlor*

The Settlor is the person who creates the trust by "settling" a sum of money or item of property on trust for the Beneficiaries.

2) *The Trustee*

The Trustee is the legal owner of the trust property, though is not the beneficial owner. The Trustee carries out all transactions of the Trust in its own name and must sign all documents for and on behalf of the Trust. Their primary duty is to obey the terms of the Trust Deed and to act in the best interests of the Beneficiaries. A Trustee can be an individual, individuals, or a Pty Ltd company, otherwise known as a Corporate Trustee.

3) *The Appointor*

The Appointor is the person named in the Trust Deed who has the power to remove and appoint Trustees. This would commonly occur when:

- The Trustee dies, becomes bankrupt or is incapacitated.
- In the case of a company, if the company is wound up.

4) *The Beneficiaries*

The Beneficiaries are the people (including entities) for whose benefit the Trustee holds the Trust property. A Discretionary Trust usually has a wide range of Beneficiaries including relatives, companies and other Trusts. The Beneficiaries of a Discretionary Trust do not have an interest in the assets of the Trust, but rather a right to be considered until the Trustee exercises its discretion to make a distribution.

The General Beneficiaries are those named in the Trust Deed who are eligible to receive a distribution of income or capital at the discretion of the Trustee (subject to the approval of the Appointor). The Remainder Beneficiaries are those who are automatically entitled to receive a proportionate distribution of income or capital to the extent that the Trustee has not otherwise exercised its discretion.

Why would you use a Discretionary Trust?

- Given tax benefits and flexibility.
- Asset protection afforded by a Trust.
- Estate planning considerations.
- Land holdings.

As a general rule, Trusts are a more tax-effective structure as a holding entity for investments, commercial real estate and other fixed assets. This is because the government decided that, from September 1987, they would tax capital gains on the disposal of assets (other than personal assets and your principal place of residence).

Individuals are provided with a 50% exemption from capital gains tax, which applies to a Discretionary Trust where the potential Beneficiaries are all individuals (not companies). Companies receive no such exemption.

Income:

A Discretionary Trust allows the Trustee flexibility in determining which Beneficiary receives an income from the activities of the Trust each year. This allows a gift of income to be made at reduced tax rates where there is a disparity in the income of the Beneficiaries.

An example of how this may apply:

Troy and Brooke: The Trust owns investment properties and receives income from those properties. Troy is currently a stay-at-home Dad, at least for the next year. Although when he returns to work, he will be on a large income of circa $500,000. Brooke is a director of EY accounting and earns $350,000. The income from the Trust generated from the investment properties would be best distributed to Troy now. In the future, when Troy returns to work, they can change the distribution of income to be relevant to their circumstances.

*****Please note:** *You should consult your accountant and seek specific advice on your circumstances before making any decisions relating to your taxation requirements.*

Asset protection:

The Trustee of a Discretionary Trust holds the property for the Beneficiaries. Property held by a Trustee cannot be taken by a creditor in bankruptcy unless the debt is a Trust debt. Similarly, a property held by a company as the Trustee cannot be taken by creditors in a liquidation of that company unless the debt is a debt of the Trust.

Testamentary Trusts

A Testamentary Trust is a Trust set out in a Will that only takes effect when the person who has created the Will dies. That is, the Trust commences on death. Testamentary Trusts are usually set up to protect assets.

Here are some reasons why you would create a Testamentary Trust:
- The Beneficiaries are minors (under 18 - 21 years old).
- The Beneficiaries have a diminished mental capacity.
- You do not trust the Beneficiary to use their inheritance wisely.
- You do not want family assets split as part of a divorce settlement.
- You do not want family assets to become part of bankruptcy proceedings.

A Trust will be administered by a Trustee who is usually appointed in the Will. The Trustee must look after the assets for the benefit of the Beneficiaries until the Trust expires.

The expiry date of a Trust will be a specific date such as when a minor reaches a certain age or a Beneficiary achieves a certain goal or milestone (e.g. getting married or attaining a specific qualification).

Estate planning

Below is an example that relates to a situation that may arise for some families:

A mum and dad die leaving one son who is a bankrupt. They leave all of their assets to him and their entire estate is lost to the Trustee in bankruptcy. Had they left their estate to a Discretionary Trust established for the benefit of their son and his family, the estate would have been saved. Alternatively, with proper estate planning, the assets could have been protected well before their death.

Estate planning paperwork

Once your paperwork is in order, it will help your Executor and family if you list the legal documents you have and where they are kept. Keeping a record of your personal information and notes on how your legal documents, assets and investments are arranged can also help you. It isn't just important to have a valid Will and power of attorney and your affairs in order, but also to make sure the documents can be easily located.

Here is a list of key documents to keep:

- Birth certificate.
- Marriage certificate.
- Will.
- Enduring power of attorney.
- Advance healthcare directive (also called a living Will).
- Personal insurance policies.
- House deeds.
- Home and contents insurance.
- Deeds and insurance policies for any other real estate you own.
- Bank account details.
- Superannuation papers.
- Investment documents (securities, share certificates, bonds).
- Medicare card.
- Medical insurance details.
- Pensioner concession card.
- Any pre-payments of funeral investments.

Setting up a Will

What is a Will?

A Will is a legal document that clearly sets out your wishes for the distribution of your assets after your death. Having a clear, legally valid, and up-to-date Will is the best way to ensure that your assets are protected and distributed according to your wishes.

Many Australians do not have a current Will. If you die without a Will, no-one knows what you wanted to do with your assets, otherwise known as your estate. Your assets will be distributed according to a set formula as present in your state of residence, with certain relatives receiving a defined percentage of your assets. The process of administering an estate when a person dies without a Will (intestate) tends to be more difficult.

Your Will is an important document, so it's best that you have it prepared by an expert who is supported by taxation and legal professionals.

For a Will to be valid it needs to comply with certain criteria:

- Unless married, you must be over 18 years old (The Supreme Court can approve a Will for people under 18 only in exceptional circumstances).
- It must be in writing – it can be handwritten, typed or printed.
- It must be signed by the person making the Will and witnessed by two or more witnesses (Beneficiaries should not be a witness as it may cancel out their entitlement).
- You must have **testamentary capacity**, meaning:
  - You know the legal effect of a Will.
  - You must be aware of the extent of your assets.
  - You must be aware of the people who would normally be expected to benefit from your estate.
  - You must not be prevented from reaching rational decisions as to who is to benefit from your Will by mental illness or mental disease.

A Will takes effect when you die. It can cover things like how your assets will be shared, who will look after your children if they are still young, what Trusts you want established, how much money you'd like donated to charities, and even instructions about your funeral.

Your Will can be written and updated by Private Trustees and solicitors, who usually charge a fee. Some Public Trustees will not charge to prepare or update your Will, but only if they act as the Executor of your Will. Other Public Trustees may only exempt you from charges if you are a pensioner or aged over 60. Check with the Public Trustee in your state or territory.

It's estimated that nearly half of all Australians die without a Will or "intestate". Don't let this happen to you. Please make sure that you have a valid Will in place.

You can buy Will kits online but it's a good idea to ask a solicitor to review your Will to make sure everything is in order. If a Will isn't signed and witnessed properly, it will be invalid.

Keep your Will valid and up-to-date as your legal rights change. If you marry, divorce or separate, have children or grandchildren, if your spouse or Beneficiaries die, or if you have a significant change in financial circumstances, you should review your Will.

As mentioned, if you die without a Will, you die intestate. This means that, since you didn't have a Will, no-one knows who you wanted as your Beneficiaries and who you wanted as your Executor. An administrator appointed by the court will pay your bills and taxes from your assets and the remainder will be distributed according to a pre-determined formula with certain family members receiving a defined percentage of your assets despite what you may have wished.

Dying intestate can result in your surviving spouse, family and friends suffering unnecessary financial hardship and emotional stress. If you are in a de-facto or same-sex relationship, it is necessary to supply sworn evidence that the relationship existed.

Executors

One of the most important decisions in preparing your Will involves determining who the Executor will be. Your Executor will be responsible for managing your estate when you have passed away, carrying out your directives and following proper legal procedures. Consider how well the individual you choose will be capable of carrying out your instructions and act in your best interests. Let your Executor know where to locate your Will upon your death. It is also possible to appoint a professional as your Executor, such as a professional Trustee company.

Powers of attorney

Appointing someone as your power of attorney gives them the legal authority to look after your affairs on your behalf.

Powers of attorney depend on which state or territory you are in – they can refer to just financial powers, or they might include broader guardianship powers. You will need to check with your local Public Trustee.

Generally speaking, there are three different types of powers of attorney:

- A **general power of attorney** is where you appoint someone to make financial and legal decisions for you, usually for a specified period of time. For example, if you are overseas and unable to manage your legal affairs at home for a set time. This person's appointment becomes invalid if you lose the capacity to make decisions for yourself.

- An **enduring power of attorney** is where you appoint a person to make financial and legal decisions for you if you lose the capacity to make your own decisions.

- A **medical power of attorney** can make only medical decisions on your behalf if you become unable to do so yourself.

You can prepare a few other documents to help your legal appointees and family as you grow older, including:

- An **enduring power of guardianship** that gives a person the right to choose where you live and make decisions about your medical care and other lifestyle choices if you lose the capacity to make your own decisions.

- An **anticipatory direction** records your wishes about medical treatment in the future in case you become unable to express those wishes yourself.

- An **advance healthcare directive (or living Will)** documents how you would like your body to be dealt with if you lose the capacity to make those decisions yourself.

The documents you choose to draw up will depend on your situation and the responsibilities that you are happy to entrust to others. Get legal advice if you are not sure.

Choosing your powers of attorney:
Nominate people that you know are trustworthy, financially astute if possible, and likely to be around when you need them. Therefore, consider the age of potential powers of attorney relative to your age.

Common questions about Wills

Where should I keep my Will?
Most people realise the importance of making a Will. A Will can only be used if it can be found when required. It is important to store your original Will in a safe place and tell someone close to you where it is stored. There have been many instances where family and friends were aware that a Will existed but they were unable to locate it when required.

How often should my Will be revised or updated?
Your Will expresses your wishes at a particular point in time. It is advisable to regularly review your Will, particularly when your circumstances change. Key events that should trigger a review of your Will include:
- Marriage.
- Separation or divorce.

- Starting a de-facto relationship.
- Having children or grandchildren.
- Your children having remarried or divorced and may have extended families.
- The Executor named in the Will, having become ill, is unable to handle the responsibility, or has died.
- A Beneficiary named in the Will has died. When writing your Will, it is wise to name substitute Beneficiaries.
- Death of spouse.
- The value of legacies diminishing over time. While you may have left a sum of money that seemed significant when you last made your Will, what is it worth in **today's** dollars?
- Retirement often results in people restructuring their affairs. This is an ideal time to be proactive in your estate planning and possibly look at setting up tax-effective arrangements through your Will.
- When you buy or sell assets. There are many examples of people bequeathing assets which they sold before they died, resulting in some Beneficiaries receiving nothing while others received significantly more than was intended in the original Will.

As a guide, reviewing your will every 5 years or when one of the events above occurs is good practice.

If I get married or divorced does that affect my Will?

If you marry after you have made a Will, the Will is generally revoked, unless it was made in anticipation of marriage. Marriage will not affect a gift to the person who is your spouse at your date of death. If you divorce after you make your Will, it revokes or cancels any gift to a former spouse. It also cancels your spouse's appointment as Executor, Trustee or Guardian in the Will, but will not cancel an appointment of a former spouse as Trustee of property left on Trust for Beneficiaries that include children of both you and your former spouse. However, this won't apply if the Court is satisfied that the Will-maker did not intend to revoke the gift or appointment through divorce. Those issues require specific legal advice.

More about investments

Why are managed funds widely used?

1) It's easy to diversify your investments and you have access to different asset classes, companies, industries, sectors and countries.

2) Experts manage your money. The qualified investment professionals managing your money have access to information, research and robust investment processes not easily available to individuals. It's important to select high-quality investment managers.

3) It's easy to reinvest your investment earnings and take advantage of compounding. Over the long term, this compounding effect could mean a huge difference in your investment returns.

4) It's easy to set up a regular investment plan. You can choose small monthly amounts and transfer your

payments on the day you get paid as an automated form of investing.

5) You can invest for income, growth or both. The returns you get from a managed fund usually come in two forms: income (paid to you as a distribution) and capital growth (achieved only when the unit price increases in value).

6) Depending on the fund, you can start investing with small amounts such as $1,000 in a diversified way.

When evaluating managed funds, it is important to evaluate the net return or the return after fees.

Superannuation

What is the government co-contribution scheme?

Each year, courtesy of the government, you get the opportunity to potentially boost your super provided that your income falls within a low-income category. If you earn more than this, you won't be eligible. It can be relevant if you have one spouse earning a strong income and the other just working one day a week.

If you earn less than the income limit for co-contributions and make non-concessional contributions to your super, you may be entitled to receive up to $500 in co-contribution payments from the government. Eligible members earning up to the lower threshold will receive a maximum entitlement of $500. For those on incomes above the lower threshold, the benefit works on a sliding scale, phasing out at the income limit. Because these income limits can potentially change over time, double-check current rules at the time of reading to determine eligibility. At the time of writing, the income limit is $49,488 and the lower threshold is $34,488.

Note: this information is likely to be updated every couple of years, so it's a good idea to check that you have current limit information.

Government co-contributions may be available provided you:

- Made personal contributions to your super from your post-tax income.
- Earned a total income of less than the income limit in the financial year (total income is assessable income plus reportable fringe benefits and reportable employer superannuation contributions).
- Have lodged an income tax return for the financial year.
- Do not hold an eligible temporary resident visa at any time during the financial year.
- Are less than 71 years old at the end of the financial year that the contribution was made.
- Earned 10% or more of your total income for the financial year from eligible employment.

Spouse super contributions and tax offset:

Where one spouse isn't working for an extended period, you can do after-tax spouse super contributions, which provides contributions to your spouse's account with you as the contributor. The government offers a spouse tax offset of up to $540 on post-tax spouse contributions made to your spouse's super account up to the maximum income limit.

For example, if Max made a spouse contribution to Lucy's account when she was at home after having a child, he would be able to claim an 18% tax offset on the first $3,000 of contributions made to Lucy's account each financial year, provided she is earning anything from $0 up to the maximum income limit.

To maximise this offset, $250 per month or $3,000 a year contributed to your account potentially provides you with up to a $540 tax offset. Remember that a tax offset is different to a tax deduction. A tax offset actually reduces the amount of tax you pay.

Some eligibility conditions need to be met when claiming the spouse tax offset (current at the time of writing):

- ♦ You must not have claimed these contributions as a tax deduction (e.g. contributions done for Lucy as a spouse contribution).
- ♦ Both of you must be Australian residents when the contributions were made.
- ♦ You were not living separately and apart on a permanent basis.

- The sum of the assessable income and reportable fringe benefits for your spouse (e.g. Lucy) was less than the maximum income limit. The maximum income limit for 2017-18 is $40,000.

Again, remember that contribution eligibility and rules **can also change**. So, please ensure that you source the correct information when you need it.

Insurance

Here are some **insurance terms** commonly used, to help with understanding the area.

Premium:
With these insurances, the premium is the cost of insurance cover. This can be paid in different frequencies, with most paying monthly or annually.

Indexation:
Indexation on this type of insurance provides an automatic increase in your level of cover each year to keep up with inflation. You can have the choice of stepped verses level premiums. If they are stepped premiums, you will find that your premiums will increase over time.

Loadings and exclusions:
In some cases, an insurer will apply loadings or exclusions to a policy. A loading is an increase in the premium due to

a pre-existing condition (e.g. a medical condition) or where there is a higher probability of a claim (e.g. if you are a smoker). An **exclusion is something that is excluded from cover under a policy**, such as a right knee exclusion. In most cases, you would not be able to make a claim for illness, injury or death resulting from an excluded activity.

Waiting period:

This refers to the number of days that need to pass before the insurer will commence payment under an income protection claim. The waiting period may vary from one policy to the next and, in some cases, you can nominate for a longer waiting period in exchange for lower premiums on your policy. The standard waiting period for income protection is 30 days, though this can be varied and should ultimately match your needs.

Underwriting:

The process of underwriting enables the insurer to assess the risk of a client and determine the level and terms of any cover provided to them. Underwriting generally involves completing a questionnaire, providing medical evidence and, in some cases, a medical examination. It is not always required to do medical exams and it isn't a mandatory requirement. It is very important to provide all the relevant information as the insurer will have access to your full Medicare-related medical information at the time of a claim. If you withhold information, this may very likely have a negative outcome should you wish to eventually claim on your policy. **So, you really need to make sure that you disclose everything that is relevant because they will have full access at claim time anyway.**

Certificate:

This is a document issued by an insurer when you purchase an insurance policy. It is used to verify its existence and is for your record-keeping. The certificate includes the policy identification details, effective dates for the policy, type of insurance cover and the amount of cover. When you get a certificate for insurance, it's a good idea to store it in a safe place in your records and keep it there.

Index

A
Annuities, 125

D
Discretionary Trusts, 130

E
Estate planning, 100, 137

F
Family protection and insurances, 96
Fixed-interest investments, 72

I
Investing in shares, 66

L
Life expenditure plan, 20, 112

M
Managed funds, 58, 147
Money tips to live by Money manifesto, 13

P
Portfolio drawdown, 73
Powers of attorney, 142
Property and infrastructure, 70

S
Superannuation, 83, 148

T
Teaching kids money habits, 93
Testamentary Trust, 134
Things to consider in buying a home, 75
Trusts, 129

U
Using money effectively, 36

W
Wills, 144

www.ingramcontent.com/pod-product-compliance
Lightning Source LLC
Chambersburg PA
CBHW032041290426
44110CB00012B/896